EMERIL'S
CREOLE
CHRISTMAS

also by

EMERIL LAGASSE

Louisiana Real & Rustic
Emeril's New New Orleans Cooking

EMERIL'S CREOLE CHRISTMAS

EMERIL LAGASSE

with

Marcelle Bienvenu

Photographs by Christopher Hirsheimer

William Morrow and Company, Inc.

New York

LIBRARY OF CONGRESS CATALOGING-IN-PUBLICATION DATA

Lagasse, Emeril.

Emeril's Creole Christmas / by Emeril Lagasse with Marcelle Bienvenu.—

1st ed.

p.   cm.

Includes index.

ISBN 0–688–14691–0

1. Christmas cookery—Louisiana—New Orleans.   2. Cookery, Creole—

Louisiana—New Orleans.   I. Bienvenu, Marcelle.   II. Title.

TX739.2.C45L34   1997

641.5'68—dc21

97-15138

CIP

PRINTED IN THE UNITED STATES OF AMERICA

First Edition

2   3   4   5   6   7   8   9   10

BOOK DESIGN BY JILL ARMUS

To my mom,

HILDA LAGASSE,

who has inspired me since I was born. I thank her for

her constant love, support, spirit, and eternal friendship.

Without her, I would not have the wealth of memories that

stimulated me to write this book.

I look forward to accumulating more memories as

we share the passage of our life together.

Thanks, Mom, and God bless!

....

In Memory

HUGH HOHN,

a great human being, husband, father, and friend

ACKNOWLEDGMENTS

Tremendous thanks to the staffs at Emeril's, NOLA,
and Emeril's New Orleans Fish House for their continual support.
May all of you have a merry Christmas each and every year.

◆

SPECIAL, SPECIAL THANKS

To my family, whose Christmas memories live on and on, and whom I can always count on.

To Marcelle Bienvenu, a dear friend, historian, foodie, great cook, and incredible writer who always
believes in me, and to her husband, Rock the Man.

◆

To the tasters at Homebase.

◆

To Marti Dalton, my right hand and much more, who is always there through rain or shine,
and who thinks there is never a task too big to tackle.

◆

To Beth Lott, Mauricio Andrade, Tony Cruz, and Eric Linquest, who always make it happen.

◆

To Kathleen Hackett, Pam Hoenig, and all the people at William Morrow.

◆

To all the children and their parents who joined us at City Park to see the Christmas lights.

◆

To all the friends and relatives who partied on the streetcar.

◆

To Christopher Hirsheimer, the photographer for this book, who has a brilliant eye and great patience.
The photographs are fantastic.

◆

To Melange Sterling, for their graciousness and generosity.

◆

To the Private Connection, for their cooperation.

◆

To Jeff Farr with Gay Nineties Carriages, and his horse Nadine.

◆

To Brian and Shelly Smale, my great friends,
who give so much energy behind the camera that carries through to the front.

◆

To Cary Alden at The Fairmont Hotel in New Orleans.
To Coleman E. Adler & Sons, for supplying us with all that we needed and more.

◆

To Angele Parlange, a fantastic designer.

◆

To Glenn Vesh at Perfect Presentations, for his incredible flowers and Christmas decorations.

◆

To Chefs de Cuisine Bernard Carmouche, David McCelvey, and Michael Jordan,
and to pastry chefs Lou Lynch and Joe Trull.

◆

To Greg Harrington, the Master Sommelier at Emeril's.

◆

To Jessica Lagasse, my daughter.

◆

To my other daughter, Jillian Lagasse, who apprenticed in the test kitchen for this book.
May she always enjoy preparing holiday food.

◆

And finally, to my amazing assistant, Felicia Willett, for her constant dedication to this book. She kept us on
course through the shopping, testing, writing, and styling of it and kept on smiling.

◆

Thanks to you all!

MOTTO

If you could just open one

CONTENTS

INTRODUCTION

I KNEW the holidays were approaching as soon as Mom began gathering her stash of walnuts. She always enlisted my help to crack, shell, and store the nuts, which would later be used for making candies and cakes. Then she and I began the task of macerating fruits for a multitude of fruitcakes that she would present as gifts for relatives and friends.

But the biggest sign that the holidays were just around the corner was visits by Uncle Sylvester. He was big on the holidays. It was his job to make sure that we had all the supplies for setting up the bar, and that everyone in the family had been invited to our Christmas Eve party. On some of those visits, Uncle Sylvester brought along his guitar or banjo and played a couple of Portuguese tunes in the kitchen while he nipped on the Portuguese wine that had been aging in big jugs since late summer. While he strummed, Mom and I rattled around the big kitchen, stirring pots of soup and baking huge quantities of cookies and breads.

In between the cooking and baking, all sorts of activities filled the days leading up to the actual celebration of the holidays.

I was not only involved in assisting Mom but also with my second love, music. When I was a youngster, about twelve years old, I received the sublime compliment of being chosen to play the drums in St. Anthony's Band. This was a Portuguese band that played at outdoor concerts during the summer and I was very pleased with myself, but even more so during the holidays. It was during the Christmas season that I really enjoyed playing with the band. You see, the band leader had us decorate an old flatbed truck that took us from house to house playing Portuguese Christmas music. When we were invited to come in out of the cold, I got the opportunity to taste the treats of other families. I was curious about food even back then.

But most of the highlights of the season were centered at home. Mom's stove barely had time to get cold in between her baking and cooking for all the festivities. By the time Christmas rolled around, tins and boxes filled with chocolate fudge, salted nuts, butter cookies, and those fruitcakes were stacked in what we called "the entry." As I recall, it was a huge closetlike place, and I loved watching Mom as she put her stashes there.

Like all children, I was nearly wild with anticipation as the big day approached. Aunts, uncles, cousins, and a slew of friends were expected to join us Christmas Eve. We decorated the tree, piled our gifts under it, and brought out the array of food that had been put by for the occasion.

All day on Christmas Eve, excite-

ment built to a crescendo. By nightfall, it was nothing to have forty people in the house, everyone talking at once, kissing, hugging, eating, drinking. Friends, neighbors, uncles, aunts, and cousins were everywhere! Platters of spicy chicken, bowls of steam-

ing kale soup, and baskets piled with breads were passed round and round until everyone had their fill. Uncle Sylvester strummed his banjo, people joined in singing old songs, and a couple or two jigged around the kitchen table.

Looking back, I know now how I learned the lesson of sharing, no mat-

ter how simply, with the people we love. To be sure, food was, and still is, the focus of this sharing. Everyone went home with a little something that my mother and I had lovingly prepared.

Now, in my adopted hometown, New Orleans, where I've been living for fifteen years, I've added another chapter of memories to those I recall so fondly every year.

My first Christmas in the Crescent City, where the temperature struggles to dip below sixty degrees, was a little unsettling. Yet it was exciting to experience the holidays in a subtropical climate where Christmastime is enjoyed beside banana plants and camellia bushes. My daughters, Jessica and Jillian, were toddlers when we moved south and it was a special time for all of us. I've always enjoyed fatherhood, but especially so at Christmas. Once they were put to bed, Santa had his work cut out. For Jillian there were always a collection of dolls, and one year I had a heck of a time setting up her Barbie dollhouse. Jessica's passion leaned toward musical toys. I almost went deaf the year Santa brought her a small organ. Both adored storybooks and I came to know many by heart after reading them over and over to them.

Early on they were introduced to the accoutrements of cooking. They had tea sets, a small wooden table on which to put them, and a toy stove and sink to go along with their kitchen arrangement.

Christmas morning was as much a joy to me as it was for them. They squealed in delight with the opening of each present. What fun we had!

I became quickly acclimated to New Orleans, a city of celebrations with customs and traditions that are steeped in history. With its powerful French and Spanish backgrounds, New Orleans was, and still is, a city unlike any other in America. And the traditions, celebrations, and customs are based on this Gallic influence.

Although this port city, with its infusion of other ethnic cultures, has

long been considered a free-living, roaring, flamboyant (and to some very wicked) place, it is one that sustains an incredibly strong belief in religion and the outward demonstration of it.

Christmas for many New Orleanians was, and continues to be, an occasion for religious observance, particularly among the large Catholic community. To this day, throngs gather, as they have since 1794, at grand St. Louis's Cathedral in the heart of the French Quarter to attend the solemn and impressive Midnight Mass on Christmas Eve.

After Mass, many of the old New Orleans families continue the tradition of celebrating with a supper, or *reveillon,* with menus that include old favorites like grillades (a Creole dish of pieces of pounded veal or beef braised in a rich gravy made with onions, bell peppers, celery, tomatoes, and herbs and spices) and grits, glazed hams, hot biscuits, and cornbread that are sometimes served along with more contemporary fare.

For many Louisiana French families, Christmas Eve and Christmas Day festivities have always been dedicated to the immediate family and the many relatives who traveled in from the country to spend the season in the city. It was a time for visiting, feasting, and exchanging small gifts. The children received small trinkets, such as French-made mechanical toys and tiny dolls, and homemade delights—pralines, toasted pecans, candied fruit—wrapped in tissue and tied with dainty ribbons.

In the nearby rural communities, countrymen took advantage of the few days of leisure by hunting. Their trophies of rabbit, wild ducks and geese, and deer were brought home to be roasted, baked, or plunked in the gumbo pot, all accompanied by Acadian favorites like baked sweet potatoes, mirliton and shrimp casseroles, and mounds of rice dressing and cornbread dressing flavored with oysters, if some were to be had. Their celebration too was deeply rooted in family customs. Handmade dolls, hand-carved toys, and bags of oranges were gifts for the young, em-

broidered handkerchiefs and fanciful shawls were given to the ladies, and the gentlemen might be presented with cigars and good whiskey.

Along the Mississippi River, in what is now called the River Parishes (counties are called parishes in

Louisiana), great bonfires burned on the eve of Christmas to light the way for Papa Noël while the locals feasted on a variety of gumbos and jambalayas.

Whereas Christmas Day in the city was passed in relative quiet, New Year's Eve and New Year's Day were considerably more festive.

New Year's Eve was celebrated with singing and dancing. Fireworks in the streets sounded the coming of the new year, and people toasted each other on the galleries and in their tree-shaded courtyards.

Grand gifts, many imported from France and other European countries, were exchanged on New Year's Day. Friends called upon friends, then settled down to a grand feast at the end of the day.

Now that I've celebrated the holidays here for more than a decade, I've realized that many of these traditions and customs are still followed by the old New Orleans families. But there are also new celebrations that I have come to know and love. I look forward to the candlelight caroling held in Jackson Square, outdoor choir concerts, Christmas tree lightings uptown and downtown, the majestic Celebration in the Oaks lighting dis-

play at City Park, steamboat cruises on the mighty Mississippi, buggy rides through the French Quarter, and, of course, all the incredible food that can be enjoyed not only in the many restaurants and corner cafés of the city but also in people's homes, where everyone is welcomed with open arms—all the time.

This is a city that has a hypnotic charm of its very own, where socializing and entertaining are a way of life. It's my kind of town!

I noticed early on that the ingredients used in Louisiana are not unlike those that we had in Fall River, Massachusetts. Mom used onions, bell peppers, garlic, parsley, and a generous hand with herbs and spices in her pots, much like the people do here. We had "favish," a dish made with fava beans; here they have red beans. We had walnuts, while they have pecans. Same thing, right? Well, it's mighty

close! I quickly felt right at home here, so much so that I moved Mom and Pop to New Orleans and they've blended right in.

Our celebrations revolved around the family and the table, just as they do here. I have never seen so many aunts, uncles, cousins, and grand-

parents. Why, my friend Marcelle has over thirty first cousins, and that's just on the Bienvenu side of her family!

Christmas Day at our house is not unlike many of yours, except that here we have a meal that lasts all day. I certainly found my niche in this city

where food is the center of the culture. Like a lot of other people here, I just can't seem to stop cooking and enjoying watching others eat.

That's what inspired me to write this book. The holidays have always been my favorite time of year. I like to be surrounded by the people I love and enjoy a good meal—well, maybe not just a good one, more like an incredible one. I always like to kick things up a notch, but during the holidays, hey, I kick them up two, three, maybe four notches.

Take, for example, a tradition that I've started: Friends and I rent a streetcar, decorate it with garlands and big red bows, pick up guests along the route, and munch caviar and sip champagne. We rumble down St. Charles Avenue, through the Central Business District twinkling with thousands of colorful lights, then up the Avenue, skirting the Garden District, where magnificent mansions are splendidly decorated with drapes of native magnolia branches and bright red camellias. Then it's back home to enjoy a steaming hot crab bisque, baked ham, crawfish pies, and anything else that I can manage to whip up.

I feel blessed to be able to participate in the *joie de vivre* of this great city. That is why I wanted to share with you some of the *specialités* and treats that I've created for my holiday feasting.

Within these pages, there's something for everyone. You'll find some Creole favorites, such as rich, creamy eggnog and Creole Christmas Fruitcake with Whiskey Sauce. Or maybe your taste buds will be tingled with dishes like Smothered Grits with Crawfish or Spicy Crab Cakes with Fried Quail Eggs that were inspired by my country friends in Acadiana.

From my childhood memories, I've re-created old favorites like Mixed Nut Brittle and Big Boy Cookies. When my imagination ran wild, I concocted Truffle Potato Soup with Truffle Mushroom Dumplings and Oyster and Parsley Chowder.

If you can't come over to my house, you'll be able to fix these and a whole lot more fantastic dishes at yours. It's my holiday wish that the recipes in these pages become part of your holiday tradition. Just

think—maybe someone's holiday memories will be made by your gift of something prepared from this collection. I hope so.

Just as my parents influenced my passion for this season, I hope that *Emeril's Creole Christmas* jump starts your creative juices.

Joyeux Noel and Bonne Année!

Emeril Lagasse

A WORD FROM MASTER SOMMELIER GREG HARRINGTON

The holidays are a time for celebration. For me, wine is always a part of this celebration. Wine is meant to be experienced with others, as part of a meal. Yet so many people haven't experienced wine's great pleasures, which bothers me. Wine can be compared to music —layered and complex, but at the same time simple to enjoy.

Just as you don't have to be a concert pianist to enjoy music, you don't have to be a wine expert to enjoy wine.

Wine pairing is the art of matching wine flavors, textures, and sensations with those of food. A great food and wine pairing enhances the taste of both the food and the wine.

And wine is meant to accompany food.

Believe it or not, you are already familiar with pairings. The ritual of morning coffee is a perfect example. Coffee is a hot beverage, intense in flavor, and bitter. Milk cools the coffee and smooths the intensity of its flavor. The addition of sugar lessens the bitterness. Food and wine pairings work in much the same way. Another common example is pizza and beer. The pizza is rich and sweet; beer is acidic and bitter. The beer seems less bitter because of the sweetness of the tomato sauce.

Food and wine pairing is easy if a few rules are observed.

1. *Every wine will either compare or contrast with the food.* This is actually very simple. All dishes have one of the following predominant elements: sweet, sour, salt, and bitter.

If the matching compares, the flavors will blend. For example, if you partner sparkling wine with a vinaigrette dressing (both predominantly acidic flavors), both the food and wine will seem less acidic.

If the matching contrasts, the flavors of each will be greatly intensified. If you serve that same sparkling wine with a creamy dressing (the wine being acidic, the dressing rich), the wine will seem more acidic and the dressing richer.

2. *Match the wine with the sauce of the dish.* The sauce of a dish is the predominant flavor of that dish. Again, find the predominant flavor and match the wine with the flavor of the sauce. Grilled chicken is a straightforward match with Chardonnay, its smoky flavor harmonizing with the toasty oak flavors of the Chardonnay. However, baste the chicken with barbecue sauce and the pairing doesn't work. The flavor of the wine is lost because the sweetness of the sauce dominates the wine. A sweet barbecue sauce needs a sweet wine. *If the predominant flavor of a dish is sweetness, then a sweet wine must be matched with the food.* Every time I go to a wedding, when I am about to eat the cake someone hands me a glass of Champagne. Have you

ever seen anyone sprinkle his cake with lemon juice? Same concept.

The wine must be more acidic than the sauce or food with which it is matched. If the sauce has higher acidity, the wine will appear dull and flabby. Matching a Chardonnay with vinaigrette dressing will make the Chardonnay taste very dull. An even more extreme example: When I was nine years old, a friend dared me to eat a jar of dill pickles with a pint of milk. To this day I am not sure if that kid liked me. Bad pairing, bad idea.

3. *Food and wine flavors should be of equal intensity.* Many wines will overwhelm the flavors of certain dishes and vice versa. Match subtle flavors with subtle wines and strong flavors with strong wines. The intensity of a beef-based gumbo would overwhelm a twenty-year-old California Cabernet Sauvignon. You would not even be able to taste the wine. Substitute a three-year-old Australian Shiraz and you have a great pairing.

Even with the thousands of wines to choose from, most wine will fall into the following six categories. For each category, I have selected a few of my favorites.

CRISP WHITE WINE

Crisp white wines pair well with dishes that are highly acidic. These wines cleanse and refresh the palate. For a great match, find wines that have not been oak-aged. Wine makers sometimes age their wines in oak to develop a rich, creamy, full-bodied flavor. Also look at the alcohol content on the label. Alcohol gives a wine its body and fullness. Wines below 12.5 percent will generally be crisp, light-style wines.

■ MY FAVORITES
Champagne
Sauvignon Blanc (no oak): Sancerre, Pouilly Fumé, New Zealand, California
Pinot Gris: Italy, Alsace, Oregon

■ LOOK FOR THESE WORDS IN THE RECIPE FOR A GREAT WINE MATCH:
vinegar, lemon juice, fried, citrus

FULL-BODIED WHITE WINE

More intense dishes require more intense flavors, which can be provided by rich wines. Wines with a higher alcohol level seem heavier on the palate and are able to match intense food flavors. Look for wines above 12.5 percent alcohol and wines that have been oak-aged. A quick but general rule is that most white wines costing over $20 in retail stores, excepting sparkling wines, have been oak-aged.

Chardonnay: California, Burgundy, Australia, Italy
Sauvignon Blanc (oak-aged): Bordeaux, California
Rhône whites: Hermitage Blanc, Châteauneuf-du-Pape Blanc

■ LOOK FOR THESE WORDS IN THE RECIPE FOR A GREAT WINE MATCH: **butter, cream, aioli**

SLIGHTLY SWEET WHITE WINE/ROSÉ

Believe me, well-made slightly sweet and pink wines are not evil. The key words, however, are "well made." A well-made wine is one crafted from quality grapes using modern technol-

ogy. High acidity is the key component to these wines. They are wonderful with slightly sweet or spicy foods.

■ MY FAVORITES

German Riesling (especially from the Mosel, Rheingau, or Pfalz)
Alsace Gewürztraminer
Chenin Blanc: Vouvray, California
Tavel Rosé

■ LOOK FOR THESE WORDS IN THE RECIPE FOR A GREAT WINE PAIRING: **spicy, hot pepper, cayenne, curry, horseradish**

LIGHT RED

These are high-acid reds. They are usually full of fruit, which translates into sweetness on your palate. Light red wines are great with lighter meat and some game. Many can also be served with fish, especially grilled fish.

■ MY FAVORITES

Pinot Noir: California, Oregon
Sangiovese: Chianti, California
Southern Rhône blends

■ LOOK FOR THESE WORDS IN THE RECIPE FOR A GREAT WINE MATCH: **pork, veal, tomatoes, andouille, tamarind, Worcestershire, spicy**

FULL-BODIED RED

These are the powerhouse reds, the Godzillas of the wine world, smashing everything in their way, almost impossible to stop or overpower.

These wines are rich and slightly bitter (a.k.a. "tannic"). Tannin is a chemical component that is imparted by the skins and stems of grapes during the fermentation of high-quality red wines. It is the drying flavor you feel on your gums when you drink tea. As a wine ages, the tannic flavors will lessen. In many young wines, the tannin will dominate the wine. Matching these wines with rich dishes like beef will tame the tannic flavors of the wine. Use these wines with the richest, most adventurous dishes.

■ MY FAVORITES
*Cabernet Sauvignon: Bordeaux,
California, Washington
Pinot Noir: Burgundy,
better California Zinfandel
Syrah: Hermitage, Côte Rotie, Australia*

■ LOOK FOR THESE
BUZZ WORDS:
**beef, lamb, stewed, veal or beef
reduction**

DESSERT WINE (SWEET WHITE OR RED)

Dessert wines are a frequently overlooked closing to a great meal. A dessert wine after dinner can be very satisfying. There are thousands of such wines available, so experiment until you find something you really like. Dessert wines are very simple to pair with food. The wine must be sweeter than the dessert.

■ MY FAVORITES
*Port: tawny and ruby
Muscat: California, France
Riesling (late harvest): Germany
Sauterne*

In a pinch, when you don't have time to plan or select wines, I have a quick solution. If you are invited at the last minute to a twenty-course feast and can bring only two wines, choose Champagne and Pinot Noir. Champagne is an extremely versatile wine. Its natural high acidity and bubbles cleanse the palate. But be-

lieve it or not, most Champagnes have almost as much sugar as many dessert wines. Pinot Noir has many of the same characteristics. The Pinot Noir grape has high natural acidity. The extreme fruit flavors of Pinot seem almost sweet on the palate.

To further enhance your dining experience, buy yourself some nice glassware. Good glassware will improve the taste of your wines.

Serve red wine in a glass that has a wide bowl with heavily curved sides. Most will hold 12 to 16 ounces. This type of glass is used for wines that are fruity and aromatic such as Pinot Noir. A glass with a narrow bowl with gently curving sides can be used for red wines that are highly structured such as Cabernet or Syrah.

Serve white wine in a 10 to 12-ounce glass with a narrow bowl and straight sides to allow the wine plenty of room to breathe.

Champagne should be served in fluted glasses. The flute is the only sparkling wineglass that will preserve the bubbles, which is the essence of sparkling wines. The wine will not bubble if the glass contains soap residue.

All wines should be served slightly chilled; whites 45° to 55°F; reds 55° to 65°F. American room temperature is too hot for most wines.

As you can see, planning a wine dinner does not have to be a nightmarish experience. For me, a perfect celebration dinner has four wines: sparkling, white, red, and dessert or brandy. The wines and the food progress together, each course richer and more intense than the previous one. Learning to develop the proper progression is a little tricky at first, but the menus offered in this book are great examples.

I have suggested four wines with each menu. Good luck, don't forget to experiment, and have fun!

CHRISTMAS EVE

DINNER
FOR TEN

THE HALLS ARE DECKED,

the silver is polished and gleaming, candlelight is reflected in the cut-glass crystal, and the gifts are wrapped. The gigantic tree is profusely decorated with a myriad of tiny lights and gay-colored ribbons. It's

Christmas Eve, and anticipation and excitement are at their height.

There's still a lot of kid in me, especially on this day. I sneak and shake boxes when I'm sure no one is around. I go through my gift-giving list once more to assure myself that I've not forgotten anyone.

I associate this day with smells. The fragrance of the Christmas tree is invigorating. The aroma of cookies or bread baking makes me feel that all is safe and well in my world. The scent of the aromatic pomanders made of cinnamon, lavender, thyme, and rosemary that hang throughout the house remind me of the burning incense at church. It

MENU

Corn Cakes with Caviar and
Traditional Garnishes

◆

Truffle Risotto with Parmesan
Croutons

◆

Salad of New Potatoes and Roasted
Walnuts with Warm Bacon
Vinaigrette

◆

Beef Tenderloin with Fresh
Horseradish and Black Pepper Crust

Exotic Mushroom Bread Pudding

Emeril's Homemade
Worcestershire Sauce

Port Wine Reduction

◆

Roasted Fennel and Green Bean Relish

Fresh Cranberry Compote

◆

Chocolate Chocolate Pudding Cake
with Chocolate Ganache

Creole Christmas Trifle

gives me a sense of peace.

I always try to allow myself a little quiet time alone on this day, before the festivities begin, to remember all that has been given to me and to remind myself how fortunate I have been to enjoy good food, good friends, and good health.

And for these very reasons I like to share this meal with my immediate family and a couple of very close friends. With the table placed near the Christmas tree, the warm glow of the lights on the tree and the candlelight makes for a warm and cozy atmosphere. It's a time for reflection and contemplation with people I can share my sentimentalism with on this occasion.

WINE PAIRINGS

SMALL CAPS **SPARKLING WINE** *Champagne*
Caviar is the perfect complement for sparkling wine. The high acidity of the sparkling wine cuts through the richness of the caviar, refreshing the palate.

◆

FULL-BODIED CHARDONNAY
Burgundy (Meursault), Puligny / Chassagne Montrachet, California, Australia

Risotto is a very rich starch, and its richness requires a wine that is also very rich and full-bodied. Oak-aged Chardonnay matches it particularly well.

◆

SYRAH-BASED RED
*Northern Rhône Valley
(Hermitage / Côte Rotie), Australia*
Syrah and black pepper–crusted meats are a great combination. This dish requires a full-bodied red wine that will match both its spicy and sweet components. Wines from Syrah fit this profile.

◆

RUBY PORT
Ruby port has a minimum amount of oak aging. The wine retains a very fresh berry character with a touch of sweetness. Chocolate and ruby port are classic together. Dessert wine pairing is very simple. Just make sure the wine is sweeter than the dessert.

The menu for this evening is relatively simple. The corn cakes are similar to pancakes, but are made a little crunchy by the addition of whole corn kernels. Topping them with caviar and traditional garnishes gives them a big bam. The risotto flavored with truffles is smooth and creamy, and has quickly become a favorite in my family. I'm a big fan of Maytag blue cheese, which is made in Newton, Iowa, and I find it gives the salad just the right punch.

Anyone who knows me knows that I'm mad about beef. The tenderloin, crusted with fresh horseradish and black pepper, is a meat-lover's delight. New Orleanians like bread pudding, but they usually have one that is sweet and eaten as dessert. I've opted for a savory one, fluffy and flavored with exotic mushrooms. The mushrooms grown on a local farm were my inspiration. This pudding will knock your socks off!

Probably the only thing I like better than beef is dessert. Since it's the holidays, I've blown out all the stops. The chocolate cake with chocolate ganache has enough chocolate to sink one of those huge cargo ships that ply the waters of the mighty Mississippi. It should be more than enough to satisfy any chocolate addict.

The trifle, a holiday tradition in my family, features toasty macaroons dipped in Grand Marnier, one of my very favorite liqueurs, and layered with rich coconut cream, lots of fresh raspberries, and whipped cream. It's big, gorgeous, and a great finale to a grand meal.

After dinner, if the weather permits, and more often than not it does, I like to serve coffee and after-dinner drinks on my balcony that overlooks the Central Business District, sparkling with holiday lights. Then it's off to the land of dreams, for tomorrow, Christmas Day, will come all too quickly, but maybe not quickly enough for me.

SHOPPING LIST

FLOUR, LEAVENERS, AND OTHER BAKING AISLE INGREDIENTS

Bleached all-purpose flour (1½ cups)
Masa harina flour (½ cup)
Yellow cornmeal (¾ cup)
Baking powder (3 teaspoons)
Cornstarch (1 cup plus 2 tablespoons)
Confectioners' sugar (about 2 tablespoons)
Granulated sugar (5 cups plus 2 tablespoons)
Dark corn syrup (4 cups)
Steen's 100% Pure Cane Syrup (2 cups)
Sweetened condensed milk
(two 14-ounce cans)
Sweetened flaked coconut
(three 14-ounce bags)
Unsweetened cocoa powder (⅓ cup)
Semisweet chocolate chips (1 pound)
Semisweet chocolate squares (½ pound)
Walnut pieces (1 cup)

SPICES, DRIED HERBS, AND EXTRACTS

Salt (about ½ cup)
Black pepper (about 8 teaspoons)
Black peppercorns (2 teaspoons)
White pepper (¼ teaspoon)
Cayenne (about 3½ teaspoons)
Cloves (½ teaspoon whole cloves)
Ground cinnamon (⅛ teaspoon)
Bay leaves (6)
Capers (¼ cup)
Basil (1 teaspoon)
Garlic powder (2 tablespoons)

Onion powder (1 tablespoon)
Oregano (4 teaspoons)
Sweet paprika (2½ tablespoons)
Tarragon (1 teaspoon)
Thyme (1 tablespoon)
Pure vanilla extract (2½ tablespoons)

OILS AND VINEGARS

Olive oil (about ½ cup)
Vegetable oil (1 cup plus 2 teaspoons)
White truffle oil (about 3 tablespoons)
Walnut oil (½ cup)
Distilled white vinegar (½ gallon)
Balsamic vinegar (¼ cup)

PRODUCE

Corn (1 medium-size ear)
Spinach (one 10-ounce bag)
Green beans (tiny, about ½ pound)
Green jalapeños (4 fresh)
Exotic mushrooms (about 1½ pounds)
Parsley (1 bunch)
Carrots (6 to 7, about 1 pound)
Celery (about 4 ribs)
Fennel (1 large bulb, about 1 pound)
Fresh horseradish (about 1¼ pounds)
Red potatoes (10 small new, about 1¼ pounds)
Garlic (2 large heads)
Green onions (called scallions everywhere but in
Louisiana, 1 bunch)
Red onion (1 small)
Yellow onions (about 17 medium-size)
Shallots (2 large, about 1 ounce)
Cranberries (one 12-ounce bag)
Lemons (3 medium-size)

Orange (1 large)
Raspberries (fresh, 6 pints)

DAIRY

Large eggs (2½ dozen)
Heavy cream (3 quarts plus 1 pint)
Milk (1 quart)
Unsalted butter (1 stick, ¼ pound)
Parmigiano-Reggiano cheese (½ pound)
Blue cheese, preferably Maytag (¼ pound)

CONDIMENTS AND CANNED GOODS

Caviar (one 7-ounce tin)
Anchovy fillets (four 2-ounce cans)
Dijon mustard (about 2½ tablespoons)
Tabasco sauce (about ½ teaspoon)
Worcestershire sauce (1 teaspoon)

LIQUOR

Grand Marnier (1¾ cups)
Port wine (3 cups)

MEAT DEPARTMENT

Bacon, sliced (½ pound)
Beef tenderloin (about 3½ pounds)
Chicken bones (raw, about 4 pounds)

MISCELLANEOUS

Arborio rice (1 pound)
Orange juice (¾ cup)
Day-old white bread (18 slices)
Parchment or waxed paper

CORN CAKES WITH CAVIAR AND TRADITIONAL GARNISHES

MAKES ABOUT 32 CAKES (3 TO 4 PER SERVING)

2 tablespoons olive oil
1 cup fresh sweet corn kernels,
*   from 1 medium-size ear*
2 tablespoons minced shallots
1 teaspoon salt
⅛ teaspoon freshly ground
*   black pepper*
2 large eggs
1 cup heavy cream
¾ cup yellow cornmeal
½ cup bleached all-purpose flour
½ cup masa harina flour
2 teaspoons baking powder
⅛ teaspoon cayenne
¾ cup water
2 teaspoons vegetable oil
1 teaspoon Creole Seasoning
*   (page 30)*
Christmas Caviar Sauce (page 58)

GARNISHES
¼ cup capers, drained
2 hard-boiled egg yolks, finely chopped
2 hard-boiled egg whites,
*   finely chopped*
¼ cup chopped red onion
2 tablespoons finely chopped fresh
*   parsley leaves*
One 7-ounce tin caviar

Stocking Tips ■ Caviar is simply sieved and lightly salted fish roe. Sturgeon roe is premium and is considered the "true" caviar. The three main types of caviar are beluga, osetra, and sevruga. The best beluga sturgeon is the Malossol from the Caspian Sea. Malossol means "little salt" in Russian. Russian law states that the caviar must contain less than 5 percent salt to be called caviar. ■ Masa harina is flour made from dried masa, which are corn kernels that have been cooked in lime water. It is usually available in large supermarkets or specialty shops.

Heat the olive oil in a medium-size sauté pan over medium heat. Add the corn, shallots, ½ teaspoon of the salt, and the black pepper and cook, stirring, until the corn and shallots are tender, about 5 minutes. Remove from the heat.

Combine the eggs and cream in a large mixing bowl and whisk to blend well. Add the cornmeal, flour, masa harina, baking powder, cayenne, the remaining ½ teaspoon salt, and the water. Mix well. Fold in the corn-and-shallot mixture.

Heat ½ teaspoon of the oil in a large nonstick sauté pan over medium-high heat. When the oil is hot, but not smoking, gently drop the batter, a tablespoon at a time, into the pan. You can cook about eight cakes at a time. Cook until the cakes are lightly golden on both sides, about 1½ minutes on each side. Repeat until all of the oil and the batter are used up.

Drain the cakes on paper towels. Sprinkle with the Creole seasoning and serve warm with caviar sauce, accompanied with a tray of garnishes. These can also be prepared in advance and passed around on trays.

TRUFFLE RISOTTO WITH PARMESAN CROUTONS

MAKES 8 TO 10 SERVINGS

1 tablespoon olive oil
1 cup chopped onions
½ teaspoon salt
¼ teaspoon freshly ground white
   pepper
⅛ teaspoon freshly ground
   black pepper
6 cups Chicken Stock (page 30)
1 teaspoon chopped garlic
1 pound (2 cups) Arborio rice
⅓ pound assorted exotic mushrooms,
   such as shiitakes, chanterelles, or
   oysters, wiped clean and chopped
   (about 2 cups)
1 tablespoon unsalted butter
¼ cup heavy cream
½ cup freshly grated Parmigiano-
   Reggiano cheese
3 tablespoons chopped green onions
   (scallions), green parts only
2 tablespoons white truffle oil

Stocking Tips ■ The high-starch kernels of Arborio rice, which is an Italian-grown grain, are thicker and shorter than other varieties of short-grain rice. Arborio is traditionally used for risotto because its increased starch lends this classic dish its requisite creamy texture. ■ White truffle oil can be found in some specialty food shops or from Urbani Truffle USA (see Mail-Order Sources, page 154). If the truffle oil is omitted, you will still have a delicious risotto.

Heat the olive oil in a large sauté pan over medium heat. Add the onions, salt, white pepper, and black pepper and cook, stirring. Sauté until the onions are slightly soft, about 3 minutes. Add the stock and garlic. Bring the mixture to a boil, reduce the heat to medium, and simmer for about 6 minutes. Add the rice and simmer for 10 minutes, stirring constantly. Add the mushrooms and continue to simmer, stirring constantly, until the mixture is creamy and bubbly, about 8 minutes. Stir in the butter, cream, cheese, green onions, and truffle oil. Simmer for 2 minutes, stirring constantly. Remove from the heat and serve immediately, accompanied by Parmesan Croutons (page 31).

Salad of New Potatoes and Roasted Walnuts with Warm Bacon Vinaigrette

MAKES 10 SERVINGS

1¼ pounds new red potatoes
   (about 10 small), scrubbed
3 teaspoons salt
½ pound bacon, chopped
2 cups chopped yellow onions
¾ teaspoon freshly ground
   black pepper
1 cup walnut pieces
2 teaspoons chopped garlic
¼ cup balsamic vinegar
½ cup walnut oil
One 10-ounce bag fresh spinach,
   thoroughly washed and
   trimmed of tough stems
¼ pound Maytag blue cheese, crumbled

Stocking Tip ■ Maytag blue cheese, made in Newton, Iowa, is exceptional. The Maytag family has been making the cheese since the 1940s, and it's a world-class blue cheese from right here in America. If it's not available, another good-quality blue cheese can be substituted.

Put the potatoes in a large saucepan and add enough water to cover them. Add 1 teaspoon of the salt and bring to a boil. Let the potatoes boil until they are fork tender, about 10 minutes. Drain. Quarter the potatoes and put them in a salad bowl. Set aside.

Cook the bacon in a large sauté pan over medium-high heat until slightly crisp, about 10 minutes. Add the onions, another teaspoon of the salt, and ¼ teaspoon of the pepper. Cook, stirring until the onions are wilted and lightly golden, about 5 minutes. Add the walnuts and cook another 5 minutes, stirring often.

Remove from the heat. Add the garlic and stir the mixture for about 30 seconds. Add the vinegar and oil and mix well.

Add ½ cup of the dressing mixture and ½ teaspoon of the salt to the potatoes and gently toss to coat evenly. Transfer the potatoes to another bowl and set aside. To the salad bowl, add the spinach, the remaining 1½ cups of the dressing, and the remaining ½ teaspoon salt and pepper. Toss to coat the leaves evenly.

Divide the spinach into ten equal portions and mound in the center of each plate. Sprinkle each with equal portions of the cheese. Arrange four potato quarters around each mound. Serve immediately.

Beef Tenderloin with Fresh Horseradish and Black Pepper Crust

One 3½-pound beef tenderloin,
    trimmed of fat
1 tablespoon olive oil
1 tablespoon Creole Seasoning
    (page 30)
2 tablespoons Dijon mustard
½ pound fresh horseradish,
    peeled and grated (about 1½ cups)
½ teaspoon finely ground
    black pepper
2 teaspoons chopped garlic
½ teaspoon salt
Emeril's Homemade Worcestershire
    Sauce (page 29)
Port Wine Reduction (page 31)

Stocking Tip ■ Fresh horseradish roots are available in many supermarkets and some Asian markets. Select roots that are firm, with no sign of blemishes.

Preheat the oven to 400°F.

Rub the tenderloin with the oil and Creole seasoning. Heat a sauté pan large enough to hold the tenderloin over high heat until the pan is very hot, about 2 minutes. Sear the meat until evenly browned on all sides, about 2 minutes per side. Remove from the heat.

Line a shallow baking pan fitted with a wire rack with aluminum foil. Place the tenderloin on the rack. Rub the top and sides of the meat with the mustard.

Combine the horseradish, black pepper, garlic, and salt in a small mixing bowl. Using your hands, press the horseradish mixture evenly over the mustard on the top and sides of the tenderloin.

Roast the tenderloin for about 30 minutes for rare (120° to 125°F on an instant meat thermometer) and about 35 minutes for medium-rare (130° to 140°F on an instant meat thermometer).

Remove from the oven and rest for 5 minutes before slicing.

Drizzle the beef with the Worcestershire sauce and wine reduction.

EXOTIC MUSHROOM BREAD PUDDING

3 tablespoons unsalted butter
3 cups thinly sliced yellow onions
2 teaspoons salt
¼ plus ⅛ teaspoon cayenne
⅛ teaspoon freshly ground
   black pepper
½ pound assorted exotic mushrooms,
   such as shiitakes, chanterelles, and
   oysters, wiped clean and chopped
   (about 3 cups)
1 tablespoon chopped garlic
5 large eggs
2 cups heavy cream
¼ teaspoon Tabasco sauce
1 teaspoon Worcestershire sauce
8 slices white bread, crusts removed, cut
   into 1-inch cubes (about 4 cups)
½ cup freshly grated Parmigiano-
   Reggiano cheese
Emeril's Homemade Worcestershire
   Sauce (page 29)
Port Wine Reduction (page 31)

Preheat the oven to 350°F.

Grease a 2-quart glass rectangular pan with 1 tablespoon of the butter.

Heat the remaining 2 tablespoons butter in a large sauté pan over medium-high heat. Add the onions, 1 teaspoon of the salt, ¼ teaspoon of the cayenne, and the black pepper. Cook, stirring, until the onions are soft, about 4 minutes. Add the mushrooms and cook, stirring, until they are slightly soft, about 3 minutes. Add the garlic and cook, stirring, for 1 minute. Remove from the heat and cool.

In a large mixing bowl, whisk the eggs for 30 seconds. Add the cream, the remaining teaspoon salt, the remaining ⅛ teaspoon cayenne, the Tabasco, and the Worcestershire. Whisk the mixture until blended. Add the onion-mushroom mixture and bread cubes and mix well. Pour the mixture into the prepared pan. Sprinkle the top with the cheese.

Bake until the pudding is golden brown and bubbly, about 55 minutes. Remove from the oven and allow to cool for 5 minutes before serving.

Spoon onto serving plates, drizzle with Emeril's Worcestershire and the wine reduction, and serve.

EMERIL'S HOMEMADE WORCESTERSHIRE SAUCE

2 tablespoons olive oil
6 cups chopped onions
4 green jalapeños with stems and seeds,
   chopped (¾ cup)
2 tablespoons minced garlic
2 teaspoons freshly ground black
   pepper
Four 2-ounce cans anchovy fillets
½ teaspoon cloves
2 tablespoons salt
2 medium-size lemons, skin and pith
   removed
4 cups dark corn syrup
2 cups Steen's 100% Pure Cane Syrup
½ gallon distilled white vinegar
4 cups water
¾ pound fresh horseradish, peeled and
   grated (about 3 cups)

Combine the oil, onions, and jalapeños in a large heavy stockpot over high heat. Cook, stirring, until slightly soft, 2 to 3 minutes. Add the remaining ingredients and bring to a boil. Reduce the heat to medium-low and simmer, stirring occasionally, until the mixture barely coats a wooden spoon, about 6 hours. Strain through a fine-mesh strainer.

Spoon the hot mixture into three hot sterilized pint-size jars, filling to within ½ inch of the top. With a clean, damp cloth, wipe the rim and fit with a hot sterilized lid. Tightly screw on the metal ring. Place the jars on a rack, without their touching one another, in a deep canning kettle with boiling water to cover by 1 inch. Cover the kettle and boil for 15 minutes.

Using tongs, remove the jars from the water, place on a clean towel, and let cool completely. During the heat processing, the contents of the jars expand, forcing some of the air out. The remaining air inside contracts as it cools to create a partial vacuum, which pulls the lids tight against the jar rims. The vacuum and the lid's sealing compound maintain the seal. A popping noise after the contents have cooled indicates that the seal is complete. To test, press the center of the cooled lid. If it stays depressed, the jar is sealed. If not, refrigerate and use the contents within 2 to 3 weeks or reseal with a new flat lid and repeat the hot water bath. Tighten the rings. Store in a cool, dark place and let age for at least 2 weeks before using. Refrigerate after opening; stored in a covered jar or bottle, the sauce will keep indefinitely.

CREOLE SEASONING

MAKES ABOUT ¾ CUP

2½ tablespoons sweet paprika
2 tablespoons salt
2 tablespoons garlic powder
1 tablespoon freshly ground black
   pepper
1 tablespoon onion powder
1 tablespoon cayenne
1 tablespoon dried oregano
1 tablespoon dried thyme

Mix all the ingredients together and store in an airtight container. Can be stored in an airtight container for up to 3 months.

CHICKEN STOCK

MAKES ABOUT 5 QUARTS

4 pounds raw chicken bones,
   including the carcass and necks,
   rinsed in cool water
8 quarts water
2 cups coarsely chopped carrots
1½ cups coarsely chopped celery
2 cups coarsely chopped yellow onions
6 garlic cloves
4 bay leaves
2 teaspoons salt
2 teaspoons black peppercorns
1 teaspoon dried oregano
1 teaspoon dried basil
1 teaspoon dried tarragon

Put the chicken bones in a large stockpot and cover with the water. Add the remaining ingredients and bring to a rolling boil over high heat. Skim off any cloudy scum that rises to the surface. Reduce the heat to medium and simmer, uncovered, for 2 hours.

Strain through a fine-mesh sieve and let cool completely. Refrigerate for 8 hours or overnight. The next day, remove any congealed fat from the surface. It will keep in the refrigerator for 3 days, or can be stored in 2- or 4-cup containers in the freezer for up to 1 month.

PARMESAN CROUTONS

1 large egg
1 tablespoon fresh lemon juice
1 cup vegetable oil
1 teaspoon Dijon mustard
¼ teaspoon Tabasco sauce
¼ teaspoon salt
1 cup freshly grated Parmigiano-
   Reggiano cheese
¼ teaspoon freshly ground
   black pepper
1 tablespoon white truffle oil
   (optional)
10 slices day-old white bread,
   crusts removed

Preheat the oven to 350°F. Line a cookie sheet with parchment or waxed paper.

In a food processor or blender, blend the egg and lemon juice together for 10 seconds. With the processor running, slowly pour in the vegetable oil through the feed tube. The mixture will thicken. Add the mustard, Tabasco, and salt, and pulse once or twice to blend well.

Spoon the mixture into a small bowl and add the cheese, pepper, and truffle oil. Mix well.

Cut each slice of bread diagonally into two triangles. Spread about 1 tablespoon of the mayonnaise mixture on each triangle. Place the triangles on the baking sheet and bake until lightly golden, about 15 minutes. Serve warm.

PORT WINE REDUCTION

½ cup chopped onions
½ cup chopped carrots
2 bay leaves
3 cups port wine

Combine all of the ingredients in a medium-size saucepan over medium heat and bring to a boil. Continue to boil the mixture until it thickens and reduces to about ½ cup, about 30 minutes. Strain through a fine-mesh strainer and let cool. Use at room temperature.

ROASTED FENNEL AND GREEN BEAN RELISH

MAKES 10 SERVINGS

1 large bulb fennel (about 1 pound), trimmed, and thinly sliced
2 cups thinly sliced onions
2 tablespoons olive oil
½ teaspoon salt
¼ teaspoon freshly ground black pepper
½ pound tiny fresh green beans, blanched in boiling water for 1 minute, then shocked in a cold-water bath

Preheat the oven to 350°F.

Put the fennel and onions in a roasting pan. Add the olive oil, salt, and pepper and toss to coat evenly. Roast until soft and lightly browned, about 1½ hours. Let cool.

Combine the fennel mixture with the beans and toss to mix. Serve at room temperature.

FRESH CRANBERRY COMPOTE

MAKES ABOUT 5 CUPS

One 12-ounce bag fresh cranberries, rinsed and picked over
Strips of zest from 1 orange (about 2 tablespoons)
¾ cup granulated sugar
3 cups water
½ teaspoon pure vanilla extract
Pinch of salt
Pinch of cayenne
⅛ teaspoon ground cinnamon
2 tablespoons cornstarch
¾ cup fresh orange juice

Put the cranberries in a medium-size nonreactive nonstick saucepan. Add the zest. Peel and seed the orange, discard the white pith, and coarsely chop. Add the chopped orange to the pot of cranberries along with the sugar, water, vanilla, salt, cayenne, and cinnamon and bring to a boil over medium heat. Reduce the heat to medium-low and simmer for 10 minutes.

Dissolve the cornstarch in the orange juice. Add the mixture to the cranberries and stir to blend. Simmer another 20 minutes until the mixture is thick like syrup. Cool completely, then spoon into a decorative dish and pass at the table. Will keep for 3 days in the refrigerator.

CHOCOLATE CHOCOLATE PUDDING CAKE WITH CHOCOLATE GANACHE

MAKES ONE 9-INCH LAYER CAKE; 10 SERVINGS

FOR THE CAKE
8 eggs
1 cup plus 2 tablespoons
  granulated sugar
⅓ cup unsweetened cocoa powder
1 cup bleached all-purpose flour
1 teaspoon baking powder
2 tablespoons unsalted butter
¾ cup Grand Marnier or other
  orange-flavored liqueur

FOR THE PUDDING
4 cups heavy cream
½ cup cornstarch
1 cup granulated sugar
5 ounces semisweet chocolate chips
2 teaspoons pure vanilla extract

FOR THE GANACHE
2 cups heavy cream
½ pound semisweet chocolate
  squares, chopped

FOR THE GARNISH OR
DECORATION OF CAKE
11 ounces semisweet chocolate chips
Confectioners' sugar

Stocking Tip ■ Tempering is a technique by which chocolate is stabilized through a melting and cooling process, thereby making it more malleable and glossy. Tempering chocolate isn't necessary for most recipes, but it is often done when the chocolate is used for icing a cake such as this one.

Preheat the oven to 350°F.

FOR THE CAKE: Put the eggs and 1 cup of the sugar in a large mixing bowl, and with an electric mixer fitted with a wire whisk beat on medium-high speed until the mixture is pale yellow, thick, and has tripled in volume, about 8 minutes, using the mixer.

Sift the cocoa, flour, and baking powder together in another large mixing bowl. Add the egg mixture and fold to mix thoroughly so the mixture is smooth.

Grease two 9 × 2-inch round cake pans with the butter. Sprinkle each with a tablespoon of the remaining sugar. Pour the cake batter evenly into the pans and bake until the cakes spring back when touched, about 25 minutes.

Let cool for about 2 minutes. Using a thin knife, loosen the edges of the cakes, then flip onto a wire rack. Let cool completely.

FOR THE PUDDING: Combine ½ cup of the cream with the cornstarch in a small bowl and stir to make a paste. Combine the paste with the remaining 3½ cups cream, the sugar, the chocolate chips, and the vanilla in a large nonstick saucepan. Using a wire whisk, stir the mixture until it is well blended. Put the saucepan over medium-low heat and whisk constantly until the chocolate melts thoroughly. Cook the mixture, stirring often, until it becomes very thick, like pudding, about 25 minutes. Pour the mixture into a bowl. Cover with plastic wrap, pressing the wrap down on the surface of the pudding to keep a skin from forming. Let cool to room temperature.

TO ASSEMBLE THE CAKE: Line a baking pan with parchment or waxed paper and place a wire rack over it. Using a serrated knife, cut each cake in half horizontally. Brush the tops of three layers each with ¼ cup of the Grand Marnier. Place the bottom layer on a 9-inch round of cardboard and set it on the wire rack. Spread 1½ cups of the pudding evenly on top of the layer. Top with a second layer of cake. Spread 1½ cups of pudding evenly over it. Repeat the same process with the third layer. Top with the fourth layer. If necessary, shave off any uneven pieces of cake with a serrated knife so that it is smooth and even on all sides. Chill for 2 hours.

TO MAKE THE GANACHE: Combine the cream and chopped chocolate in a medium-size nonstick saucepan over medium heat. Stir until the chocolate is completely melted and the mixture is smooth. Remove from the heat and stir to cool, lifting the mixture out of the pot several times with a rubber spatula or wooden spoon until it cools slightly. It should be glossy and slightly thick. This is the tempering process.

Spoon the mixture onto the top of the chilled cake, allowing the overflow to drip down the sides. Cool slightly. Carefully remove the cake from the wire rack. Chill for at least 6 hours.

FOR THE GARNISH: Melt the semisweet chocolate chips in a stainless-steel bowl set over simmering water. Stir until the chocolate has melted and is smooth.

Line a baking sheet with parchment or waxed paper. Pour the chocolate onto the baking sheet and spread evenly. Let cool, then chill until it sets. Break the chocolate into pieces, like brittle. Mound the pieces on top of the cake, sticking them in at various angles. Sprinkle with confectioners' sugar. Slice and serve.

CREOLE CHRISTMAS TRIFLE

MAKES 10 SERVINGS

**FOR THE MACAROONS
(MAKES 6 DOZEN)**

10 ⅔ cups sweetened flaked coconut
   (two 14-ounce bags)
4 teaspoons pure vanilla extract
Two 14-ounce cans sweetened
   condensed milk

**FOR THE FILLING
(MAKES 8 CUPS)**

1 quart milk
2 cups granulated sugar
1 teaspoon pure vanilla extract
10 large eggs yolks, beaten
½ cup cornstarch
½ cup water
2 cups sweetened flaked coconut
2 tablespoons unsalted butter

TO ASSEMBLE THE TRIFLE

1 quart heavy cream
¼ cup granulated sugar
1 cup Grand Marnier or other orange-
   flavored liqueur
6 pints fresh raspberries, rinsed and
   patted dry

Stocking Tip ■ Make the macaroons in advance, as they have to sit out for about 12 hours to dry.

Preheat the oven to 350°F.

FOR THE MACAROONS: Thoroughly combine the coconut, vanilla, and condensed milk in a large mixing bowl. Spoon the mixture, by tablespoon, onto parchment- or waxed-paper-lined baking sheets about ½ inch apart. Bake until lightly toasted and golden, about 15 minutes.

Remove the macaroons from the oven and transfer them to a wire rack. Let cool completely. Leave them out, lightly covered with parchment or waxed paper, for about 12 hours.

FOR THE FILLING: Combine the milk, sugar, and vanilla in a large heavy-bottomed or nonstick saucepan over medium-high heat. Whisk to dissolve the sugar. When the mixture comes to a gentle boil or simmer after about 5 minutes, take 1 cup of the milk-and-sugar mixture and add it to the yolks. Whisk to blend well. Slowly add the yolks to the milk-and-sugar mixture in the saucepan, whisking constantly. Cook over medium heat until it thickens slightly, 4 to 5 minutes, whisking occasionally.

Dissolve the cornstarch in the water. Over medium heat, slowly add this mixture to the saucepan, whisking constantly for 1 minute. Using a

wooden spoon, continue stirring for about 2 minutes. Add the coconut and continue stirring for 2 more minutes. Add the butter and stir until it is completely melted and the mixture has thickened to a custard, about 2 minutes.

Pour the mixture into a glass bowl. Cover with plastic wrap, pressing the wrap down on the surface of the cus-

tard to prevent a skin from forming. Cool completely and chill for at least 4 hours.

TO ASSEMBLE THE TRIFLE: Beat the cream with an electric mixer on high speed for about 2 minutes. Add the sugar and beat until the mixture is thick and forms soft peaks, 1 to 2 minutes. Set aside.

Beat the coconut cream with a wire whisk until it is smooth. Set aside.

Pour the Grand Marnier into a small bowl. Dip each macaroon in the liqueur, submerging for 2 to 3 seconds, then transfer them to a sheet of parchment or waxed paper.

Spread 1 cup of the coconut cream filling on the bottom of a large, deep glass trifle bowl. Top the cream filling with 8 to 10 macaroons, placing them snugly against each other. Arrange 2 pints of the raspberries on top of the macaroons. Spread 2 cups of the coconut cream on top of the raspberries. Top with more macaroons, then 2 pints of raspberries. Spread another 2 cups of the coconut cream and top with the remaining macaroons and raspberries. Spread the remaining coconut cream on top of the raspberries. Mound the whipped cream evenly over the top.

Serve immediately or keep chilled until ready to serve.

EMERIL'S
CHRISTMAS DAY
BRUNCH BUFFET

IN A WORD, CHRISTMAS DAY

is chaos! From the time I open my eyes in the morning until I close them late that night, it's bedlam. Relatives and friends begin arriving early in the day bearing baskets and bags loaded with gifts and dishes of food. Children are running around like devils wanting to know when they will be allowed to open their presents. Heck, I don't blame them. Let's get on with it. Open those boxes!

In a matter of minutes, the house is close to a total wreck. Ribbons and bows are flying, children are squealing in delight, Aunt Mary is crying because Uncle Dick finally gave her the string of pearls she's been wanting for years, someone is yelling that someone's at the door.

It's times like these that I remember the Christmas I received a real, live puppy from my grandmother. I was so excited I nearly smothered the poor little thing, cuddling it close to my chest. I held it practically all day, taking only short breaks to eat.

A year later, when I was seven or eight years old, I got an Easy-Bake Oven. Now, you may think that's an odd gift for a boy, but even back then I had a yearning to bake. I drove everyone crazy with that thing!

Marcelle tells me that one Christmas many years ago, one of her little cousins drove his new tricycle right into their giant Christmas tree. No harm was done, since back then their trees were decorated not with glass ornaments but with Spanish moss that was dipped in a mixture of water and

MENU

*for 8 adults and 4 children,
or 10 adults*

◆

Noel Nog

Holiday Mimosa

Poinsettia Cocktail

◆

Andouille Cheese Bread

White Cheddar Truffle Eggs

*Sugarcane Baked Ham with Spiced
Apples and Pears*

*Gravlax with
Christmas Caviar Sauce*

Smothered Grits with Crawfish

◆

Spiced Pecans

*Creole Christmas Fruitcake with
Whiskey Sauce*

Big Boy Cookies

SETTING A TRADITIONAL BAR

MANY WOULD NEVER think of beginning a celebratory meal without their favorite cocktail. The traditional New Orleans cocktail, as with all aspects of life here, is rich in history and tradition. Local bartenders have developed a host of drinks that are very special to the hearts of New Orleanians. Emeril has concocted several of his very own for this Christmas Day brunch.

But for those who wish to imbibe other drinks, stock up your bar. Here is what you'll need:

Vodka, gin, bourbon, rum (dark, light, spiced), scotch, vermouth (sweet and dry), brandy, triple sec, grenadine fruit juices (orange, cranberry, pineapple), sodas (ginger ale, tonic, colas, lemon-lime), simple syrup (you can buy this commercially or make it by combining equal parts sugar and water in a saucepan and boiling the mixture down to a syruplike consistency)

You should also have fresh-cut fruits such as oranges, lemons, and limes, and perhaps assorted olives for martinis. Don't forget, too, to have lots of clear crushed ice on hand as well as cocktail napkins and stirrers, and make sure to have a good stash of assorted bar glasses.

Emeril prefers to use well-known brands in his bar, but you might want to experiment to find the brands that you like.

alum, then hung on the tree branches to dry. The result was that the moss was all sparkly with the crystals that form the composition of alum—potassium aluminum sulfate. I tell you, those Acadians are very creative. Alum was once widely used as the crisping agent in canning pickles, but it can cause digestive distress. But hey, it's great for making Christmas decorations!

This is the kind of day that was meant for a buffet as far as I'm concerned. People can eat in shifts or whenever they feel like it.

Christmas is not Christmas, at least in New Orleans, without frothy eggnog spiked with both brandy and bourbon. If eggnog is not your style, I'm sure that the Holiday Mimosa or Poinsettia Cocktail will suit your taste.

I got the idea for the Andouille Cheese Bread at a local festival. Small loaves of bread, called pistolettes in this part of the country, are filled with spicy sausage and white cheddar, then deep-fried. Incredible!

Everybody likes scrambled eggs. Kick them up a notch with white truffle oil and serve them on warm potato cakes. Plan on making a double batch!

Baked ham is a southern tradition. Glazed with a mixture of brown sugar, cane syrup, molasses, and spices, it smells unbelievably good while it's baking. Leftovers are ideal for making late-night sandwiches.

Gravlax, cured raw salmon, is my contribution to this primarily southern-based meal. I have always liked it, and it's even better when you make it yourself. The pinkish red color of the salmon really dresses up the buffet table.

Combine creamy grits and succulent crawfish tails, both favorites in the Deep South. I make this delicious dish not only during the holidays but whenever crawfish is available.

When I proposed making fruitcake

for dessert, everybody shook their heads in disagreement. They told me they were a little tired of the same old hard-as-brick, heavy-as-gold dense cakes. No problem. It was a challenge, but I managed to get out of the rut and came up

with these small loaf cakes, more like pound cake packed with plump fruit and assorted nuts and kept moist with a spiking of Grand-Marnier–flavored syrup. They're great for gift-giving.

The Big Boy Cookies and Spiced Pecans are perfect munchies to be set out on trays and in nut bowls to nibble on all day.

You probably think that after everyone has eaten his fill, naps are in order.

No way, not here! I like to pile everybody in a streetcar for a short ride through the downtown area, then hop off on Canal Street and head toward the French Quarter for a leisurely stroll. There the hotels and shops, homes, and art galleries are all decorated to the hilt. We can peek through the graceful wrought-iron gates and take in the wonders of tree-shaded courtyards. People on their balconies call out Christmas greetings to everyone who passes by. If there's a nip in the air, we can warm up with a cup of café au lait or perhaps coffee spiked with brandy at one of the many cozy taverns like the Napoleon House, a personal favorite.

But all good times must come to an end, or at least taper off. Back home, I unwind by admiring my gifts, recalling the moments of the day, and snacking on a ham sandwich. I know, too, that there are more good times to come in the following week that leads to New Year's.

SHOPPING LIST

FLOUR, LEAVENERS, AND OTHER BAKING AISLE INGREDIENTS

Bleached all-purpose flour *(about 3½ pounds)*
Yellow cornmeal *(¾ cup)*
Quick-cooking white grits *(1½ cups)*
Baking powder *(2 teaspoons)*
Cornstarch *(¼ cup plus 2 teaspoons)*
Dry yeast *(one ¼-ounce envelope)*
Granulated sugar *(about 4 pounds)*
Firmly packed light brown sugar *(1 cup)*
Dark corn syrup *(½ cup)*
Steen's 100% Pure Cane Syrup *(1 cup)*
Dark molasses *(½ cup)*
Almond paste *(4 ounces)*
Slivered blanched almonds *(1 cup)*
Ground pecans *(1 cup)*
Pecan pieces *(3 cups)*
Walnut pieces *(1 cup)*

SPICES, DRIED HERBS, AND EXTRACTS

Salt *(3½ tablespoons)*
Kosher salt *(2 cups)*
Black peppercorns *(2 tablespoons plus 1 teaspoon)*
Black pepper *(¼ teaspoon)*
White pepper *(about 2 teaspoons)*
Cayenne *(about 1 teaspoon)*
Dry mustard *(1 teaspoon)*
Ground allspice *(⅛ teaspoon)*
Ground cinnamon *(about 2 teaspoons)*
Ground cloves *(¼ teaspoon)*
Freshly grated nutmeg *(about 1 tablespoon)*
Bay leaves *(6)*
Capers *(¼ cup)*
Pure vanilla extract *(1 tablespoon)*

OILS

Vegetable oil *(about 3 quarts)*
Olive oil *(about ¼ cup)*
White truffle oil *(1 tablespoon)*
(optional)

PRODUCE

Carrots *(2 carrots, ⅓ pound)*
Celery *(2 ribs)*
Chives *(1 tablespoon chopped)*
Tarragon *(¼ cup chopped plus 5 sprigs)*
Dill *(½ cup chopped)*
Thyme *(10 sprigs)*
Parsley *(1 bunch)*
Garlic *(2 heads)*
Green onions *(called scallions everywhere but in Louisiana, 1 bunch)*
Red onion *(1 small)*
Yellow onions *(4 medium-size)*
Shallots *(about 4)*
Baking potatoes *(4 large, about 4 pounds)*
Granny Smith apples *(4, about 1½ pounds)*
Lemons *(4)*
Oranges *(3)*
Bartlett pears *(4, about 1½ pounds)*
Sugarcane swizzle sticks *(12)*
Assorted dried fruits, such as cranberries, blueberries, cherries, raisins, and apricots *(1 pound)*

LIQUOR

Bourbon *(1¼ cups)*
Brandy *(¼ cup)*
Grand Marnier or other orange-flavored liqueur *(about 1½ cups)*
Vodka *(¼ cup)*
Champagne *(1 bottle plus ¼ cup)*
Dry red wine *(1 cup)*

DAIRY

Large eggs *(3½ dozen)*
Half-and-half *(1½ quarts)*
Heavy cream *(1 quart plus 1 pint)*
Sour cream *(1 pint)*
Unsalted butter *(2 pounds)*
Parmigiano-Reggiano cheese *(about ¼ pound)*
White cheddar cheese *(¾ pound)*

FRUIT JUICES

Cranberry juice *(½ cup)*
Orange juice *(1 cup)*

CONDIMENTS AND CANNED GOODS

Caviar *(1 tablespoon)*
Salmon roe *(1 tablespoon)*
Wasabi-injected roe *(2 tablespoons)* (optional)
Tomato paste *(one 6-ounce can)*

MEAT DEPARTMENT

2 duck carcasses *(about 4 pounds)*
Andouille or kielbasa sausage *(½ pound)*
Hickory smoked ham *(1, spiral sliced, 8 to 10 pounds)*

FISH AND SEAFOOD COUNTER

Fresh salmon fillet *(4½ pounds)*
Crawfish tails, peeled *(1 pound)*

MISCELLANEOUS

Toasted croutons *(about 3 dozen)*
Cheesecloth
Black truffles *(optional)*

NOËL NOG

MAKES 8 TO 10 CUPS

10 large eggs
2¼ cups granulated sugar
2 cups half-and-half
2 cups heavy cream
¼ teaspoon freshly grated nutmeg plus
    some for garnish
1 teaspoon pure vanilla extract
¼ cup bourbon
¼ cup brandy
6 large egg whites

In a large, heavy-bottomed saucepan, beat together the eggs and sugar. Stir in the half-and-half. Cook over medium-low heat, stirring constantly, until the mixture is thick enough to coat a metal spoon with a thin film and reaches at least 160°F. Remove from the heat. Stir in the cream, nutmeg, vanilla, bourbon, and brandy. Cool, then cover and refrigerate until ready to serve.

Just before serving, beat the egg whites in a large bowl with an electric mixer on high speed until stiff peaks form, then fold them into the eggnog. Serve cold in punch cups and sprinkle with nutmeg.

Stocking Tip ■ It's best to serve the eggnog within 24 hours of preparing it.

HOLIDAY MIMOSA

MAKES 6 SERVINGS

6 tablespoons Grand Marnier
  or other orange-flavored liqueur
2 tablespoons granulated sugar
1 bottle chilled Champagne
1 cup fresh orange juice

Pour the Grand Marnier in a small bowl. Put the sugar in a saucer. Dip the rims of Champagne glasses first in the Grand Marnier, then in the sugar to form a crust. Fill each Champagne glass with three parts Champagne and 1 part orange juice.

POINSETTIA COCKTAIL

MAKES 1 COCKTAIL

¼ cup vodka
¼ cup Champagne
½ cup cranberry juice
Crushed ice
2 strips orange zest, each about
  ¼ inch wide and 2 inches long

Combine the vodka, Champagne, and juice in a large-stemmed red wineglass. Add crushed ice and stir until the mixture is well chilled. Twist the orange strips over the glass, drop them in, and serve.

ANDOUILLE CHEESE BREAD

1 envelope (¼ ounce) dry yeast
2 tablespoons granulated sugar
2 tablespoons plus 1 teaspoon
   vegetable oil
2 cups warm water (about 110°F)
6 cups bleached all-purpose flour
¾ cup yellow cornmeal
2 teaspoons salt
½ pound andouille or kielbasa sausage,
   chopped (about 1 cup)
½ pound white cheddar cheese, grated
   (about 1 cup)
Vegetable oil for deep frying

Combine the yeast, sugar, and 2 tablespoons of the oil in the bowl of an electric mixer fitted with a dough hook. Add the water. With the mixer on low speed, beat the mixture for about 4 minutes to dissolve the yeast. If the yeast mixture doesn't begin to foam after a few minutes, it means it's not active and will have to be replaced.

In a separate large mixing bowl, combine the flour, ½ cup plus 2 tablespoons of the cornmeal, and the salt. Add this mixture to the yeast mixture. Mix on low speed until it lightly comes together, then increase the speed to medium and beat until the mixture pulls away from the sides of the bowl, forms a ball, and climbs slightly up the dough hook.

Remove the dough from the bowl. Coat the bowl with the remaining teaspoon vegetable oil. Return the dough to the bowl and turn it to oil all sides. Cover the bowl with plastic wrap, set in a warm, draft-free place, and let rise until doubled in size, about 2 hours.

Meanwhile, brown the sausage in a medium-size skillet over medium heat for about 4 minutes. Drain well on paper towels. Set aside to cool to room temperature.

Remove the dough from the bowl and turn it onto a lightly floured surface. Using your hands, gently roll and form it into a narrow loaf about 24 inches long. Cut the dough into 18 equal portions (each about 2½ ounces). With the palm of your hand, roll the portions on a lightly floured surface to form small round rolls.

Line a baking sheet pan with parchment or waxed paper and sprinkle it with the remaining 2 tablespoons cornmeal.

Place the rolls about 1 inch apart on the paper. Using a pointed knife, make a slit in the top of each roll. With your thumb and forefinger, spread the dough open to make a small cavity about 1 inch deep and 2 inches wide. Spoon 1 tablespoon of the cheese into each cavity, then top with 1 tablespoon of the sausage, pressing the mixture gently into the cavity. Pinch the dough together to close the cavity. Cover the rolls with plastic wrap and let rise in a warm, draft-free place until doubled in size, about 30 minutes.

Heat 4 inches of oil, or enough to submerge the breads, in a deep pot or electric fryer to 360°F. Deep-fry the stuffed breads, two to three at a time, in the hot oil for about 3 minutes, turning them with a metal spoon or spatula to brown them evenly. Drain on paper towels. Serve warm.

White Cheddar Truffle Eggs

4 large baking potatoes (about
  4 pounds), peeled and grated
3 teaspoons salt
1¼ teaspoons freshly ground
  white pepper
2 tablespoons plus 2 teaspoons
  olive oil
¾ cup vegetable oil
1 dozen large eggs
1 tablespoon white truffle oil
  (optional)
¾ cup half-and-half
¼ cup chopped green onions
  (scallions), green parts only
1 tablespoon chopped fresh
  parsley leaves
1 tablespoon unsalted butter
¼ pound white cheddar cheese,
  grated (about 1½ cups)
Shaved or sliced black truffles
  for garnish (optional)

Stocking Tip ■ A truffle slicer is a small kitchen gadget with an adjustable blade mounted on a stainless-steel frame. The blade is held at a 45-degree angle and the truffle is pressed down and across it, allowing the blade to shave off small slivers and slices.

Wrap the grated potatoes in a large clean towel and squeeze out the excess starch. Get them as dry as possible. Unwrap and put the potatoes in a large mixing bowl. Add 2 teaspoons of the salt, 1 teaspoon of the white pepper, and the olive oil and toss to mix well. Form the mixture into 12 small cakes about 3 inches in diameter and 1 inch thick.

Heat the vegetable oil in a 10- or 12-inch nonstick skillet over medium-high heat until it's hot but not smoking. Fry the cakes, several at a time, until they are golden brown and cooked through, about 4 minutes on each side. Drain on paper towels and keep warm.

Pour off the oil and wipe the skillet clean. Set aside.

In a large mixing bowl, whisk the eggs until frothy, about 1 minute. Add the remaining teaspoon salt, the re-maining ¼ teaspoon white pepper, the truffle oil if using, half-and-half, green onions, and parsley. Whisk to blend.

In the skillet, heat the butter over medium heat for 1 minute. Add the egg mixture. Using a wooden spoon, stir the eggs often and cook until the mixture sets slightly, but is still soft, 7 to 8 minutes. Cook 2 to 3 minutes longer if firmer eggs are desired. Add the cheese, stir gently for about 30 seconds, and remove from heat. Continue stirring the mixture until the cheese melts completely.

To serve, top each potato cake with an equal portion of the eggs. Garnish with shaved truffles if desired. Serve warm.

Sugarcane Baked Ham with Spiced Apples and Pears

MAKES 10 TO 12 SERVINGS

12 sugarcane swizzle sticks, each cut into about 3-inch pieces
1 hickory smoked ham, spiral sliced, 8 to 10 pounds (no bone, water added, cooked)
1 recipe Spiced Glaze (page 58)
1½ pounds (about 4) Granny Smith apples
1½ pounds (about 4) Bartlett pears

Preheat the oven to 350°F.

Line a shallow baking pan with parchment or waxed paper.

Insert the sugarcane sticks into the ham at 3- to 4-inch intervals. Tie the ham, using kitchen twine, at two-inch intervals horizontally and vertically to keep it together. Place on a wire rack in the baking pan. Brush the entire ham with the glaze, coating it evenly.

Wash, core, and halve the fruit. Place all around the ham. Baste the ham a second time and baste the fruit with the glaze. Bake for 45 minutes. Baste the ham and fruit again. Bake an-

other 45 minutes. Remove the ham from the oven and let it rest for 5 minutes. Remove and discard the string and swizzle sticks.

Serve the apples and pears on a platter with the ham. Serve everything warm or at room temperature.

GRAVLAX WITH CHRISTMAS CAVIAR SAUCE

MAKES 24 HORS D'OEUVRE SERVINGS

2 cups kosher salt
2 tablespoons cracked black peppercorns
¼ cup finely chopped fresh tarragon
*   leaves*
½ cup chopped fresh dill
½ cup granulated sugar
2 tablespoons orange zest strips
*   (from 2 oranges)*
½ cup fresh orange juice
*   (from 2 oranges)*
1 teaspoon pure vanilla extract
One 4- to 4½-pound side of salmon
*   fillet, skin and pin bones removed,*
*   rinsed under cool water, and*
*   patted dry*
Christmas Caviar Sauce (page 58)

GARNISHES
Capers
Finely chopped hard-boiled egg yolks
*   and egg whites*
Finely chopped red onion
Finely chopped fresh parsley leaves
Toasted croutons

Stocking Tip ■ Zest oranges (or lemons, for that matter) over the bowl in which you mix the ingredients so that the oil from the zest permeates the mixture.

Combine the salt, peppercorns, tarragon, dill, sugar, zest, juice, and vanilla in a medium-size mixing bowl. Mix well. Set aside.

Lay a piece of plastic wrap twice the size of the salmon on a flat surface. Cross another piece of plastic of the same size over the first piece horizontally. Place the salmon in the center of the pieces of plastic wrap, with the skin side down. Spoon the seasoning mixture over the top and sides of the salmon. Using your fingers, spread the mixture evenly over the salmon. No part of the flesh of the fish should be exposed. With the palm of your hand, gently press the mixture into the salmon.

Fold the two pieces of plastic wrap very tightly around the salmon, folding in the ends securely. Wrap the salmon a second time with another large piece of plastic. Place the wrapped salmon in a shallow glass bowl and refrigerate for 24 hours.

Remove from the refrigerator and unwrap the salmon carefully. Discard the wrap and scrape off the seasoning mixture. Rinse the salmon under cold water for about 2 minutes to remove all of the seasoning mixture. Pat the salmon dry, wrap tightly in plastic wrap, and refrigerate until ready to serve.

To serve, remove 2 inches from the tail of the salmon. Slice the salmon, at an angle, into paper-thin slices. Serve with the caviar sauce and traditional garnishes.

SMOTHERED GRITS WITH CRAWFISH

MAKES 8 TO 10 SERVINGS

1 pound peeled crawfish tails
1 teaspoon salt
½ teaspoon cayenne
2 tablespoons olive oil
1 cup chopped yellow onions
1 tablespoon plus 1 teaspoon chopped
  garlic
2 cups Duck Stock (page 57)
3 cups half-and-half
1½ cups quick-cooking white grits
½ cup freshly grated Parmigiano-
  Reggiano cheese

Stocking Tip ■ Crawfish are freshwater crustaceans that resemble miniature lobsters. The peeled tail meat can be found in many supermarkets or seafood markets.

Toss the crawfish tails with the salt and cayenne in a medium-size mixing bowl.

Heat the olive oil in a 3-quart saucepan over medium heat. Add the onions and cook, stirring, until slightly soft, about 2 minutes. Add the craw-fish and garlic and cook, stirring, for 2 minutes. Add the stock and half-and-half and bring the mixture to a boil. Reduce the heat to medium-low and simmer for 2 minutes. Add the grits and stir constantly until they are tender and creamy, about 10 minutes. Add the cheese and stir to mix and melt it. Serve warm.

Duck Stock

MAKES ABOUT 4 CUPS

2 duck carcasses (about 4 pounds)
1 tablespoon vegetable oil
2 teaspoons salt
⅛ teaspoon freshly ground black pepper
1 cup chopped carrots
1 cup chopped celery
3 cups chopped yellow onions
1 head garlic, split in half
6 bay leaves
1 cup dry red wine
¼ cup tomato paste
12 cups water
10 sprigs fresh thyme
5 sprigs fresh tarragon
8 sprigs fresh parsley
1 teaspoon black peppercorns

Break and crack the bones of the carcasses.

Heat the vegetable oil in a 6-quart stockpot over medium-high heat. Season the bones with 1 teaspoon of the salt and the black pepper. Add the bones to the pot and brown for about 10 minutes, stirring often.

Add the carrots, celery, onions, garlic, bay leaves, and the remaining teaspoon salt. Cook until the vegetables are soft, about 5 minutes, stirring often.

Add the wine and tomato paste and stir to mix. Cook for 5 minutes, stirring occasionally. Add the water. Put the thyme, tarragon, and parsley sprigs in a piece of cheesecloth, tie it together with kitchen twine, and add it to the mixture. Add the peppercorns and bring the mixture to a boil. Skim off any cloudy scum that rises to the surface. Reduce the heat to medium and simmer, uncovered, for 3 hours.

Strain through a fine-mesh strainer and cool. Refrigerate overnight and remove any congealed fat from the surface. The stock can be stored in the freezer for 1 month.

CHRISTMAS CAVIAR SAUCE

MAKES 2 CUPS

2 cups sour cream
¼ cup fresh lemon juice
2 tablespoons minced shallots
1 tablespoon snipped fresh chives
1 tablespoon finely chopped fresh
   parsley leaves
1 teaspoon salt
⅛ teaspoon freshly ground
   white pepper
⅛ teaspoon freshly ground black pepper
2 tablespoons wasabi-injected roe
   (optional)
1 tablespoon caviar
1 tablespoon salmon roe

Stocking Tip ■ Wasabi is the Japanese version of horseradish that comes from the root of an Asian plant. It's made into a green-colored condiment that has a pungent flavor. Wasabi-injected roe can be purchased at Asian markets and some seafood specialty markets. If you can't get the wasabi-injected roe, omit it.

Combine all of the ingredients, except the roe, caviar, and salmon roe, in a mixing bowl and whisk to blend well. Gently fold in the roe, caviar, and salmon roe. Use immediately or store for up to 1 day in the refrigerator.

SPICED GLAZE

MAKES 2 ½ CUPS

1 cup firmly packed light brown sugar
1 cup Steen's 100% Pure Cane Syrup
½ cup dark molasses
½ cup dark corn syrup
⅛ teaspoon freshly grated nutmeg
¼ teaspoon ground cloves
⅛ teaspoon ground allspice
½ teaspoon ground cinnamon
1 teaspoon dry mustard
¼ cup water

Combine the sugar, cane syrup, molasses, corn syrup, nutmeg, cloves, allspice, and cinnamon in a medium-size bowl and mix well. In another bowl, dissolve the mustard in the water, then add to the spice mixture. Blend well.

Use immediately or store in an airtight container in the refrigerator until ready to use. Will keep for 2 weeks.

SPICED PECANS

2 cups water
2 cups plus 1 teaspoon
   granulated sugar
¼ teaspoon plus ⅛ teaspoon
   cayenne
2 cups pecan pieces
4 cups vegetable oil
½ teaspoon salt
¼ teaspoon ground cinnamon

Combine the water, 2 cups of the sugar, and ¼ teaspoon of the cayenne in a medium-size, heavy-bottomed saucepan over medium-high heat. Cook, stirring occasionally with a wooden spoon, until the mixture comes to a boil and becomes slightly thick, about 5 minutes.

Add the pecans and cook for 5 minutes, stirring often. Drain the pecans in a colander set over a bowl, shaking off the excess liquid.

Heat the oil to 360°F in a deep frying pot or electric fryer. Add the pecans and fry until they are a deep mahogany color, 4 to 5 minutes, stirring often. Remove the pecans with a slotted spoon and drain on a platter lined with parchment paper. Stir the pecans so they won't stick together.

Combine the salt, the remaining ⅛ teaspoon cayenne, the cinnamon, and the remaining 1 teaspoon sugar in a bowl. Sprinkle the pecans with this mixture. Let cool. Serve in small nut cups or decorative bowls.

They can be stored in an airtight container for up to 1 week.

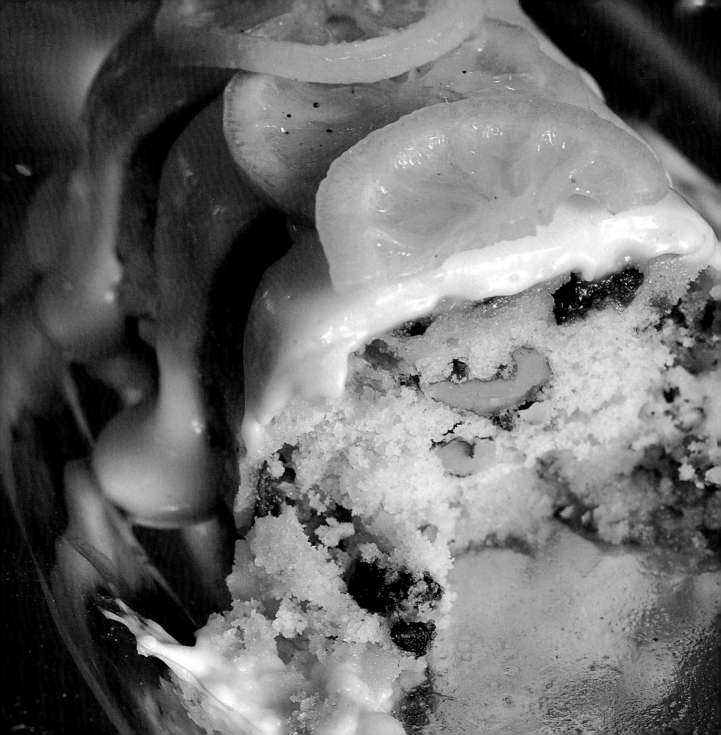

CREOLE CHRISTMAS FRUITCAKE WITH WHISKEY SAUCE

MAKES 12 CAKES

FOR THE SIMPLE SYRUP
2 cups granulated sugar
2 cups water
Strips of zest of 2 lemons
(about 3 tablespoons)
Juice of 2 lemons (about ¼ cup)

FOR THE CAKE
1 pound of a combination of dried
fruits, such as blueberries,
cranberries, cherries, raisins, and
chopped apricots
1 pound (4 sticks) unsalted butter,
at room temperature
2¼ cups granulated sugar
4 ounces almond paste
8 large eggs
1 cup Grand Marnier or other
orange-flavored liqueur
4 cups bleached all-purpose flour
2 teaspoons baking powder
¼ teaspoon salt
¼ teaspoon ground cinnamon
⅛ teaspoon freshly grated nutmeg
1 cup slivered blanched almonds
1 cup pecan pieces
1 cup walnut pieces
½ cup bourbon

Stocking Tips ■ Organize the ingredients so that everything you need will be at hand when you begin. ■ Use a fresh clove of nutmeg if possible. The essence that is released when it is grated intensifies the flavor. ■ Remember to zest the lemons over the pot so the lemon oil that is released permeates it. ■ For gift-giving, wrap each loaf in festive cellophane and tie it up with a bow or pack in holiday loaf tins. The whiskey sauce can be put into small jars and refrigerated for up to 24 hours. The sauce should be reheated at serving time.

Make a simple syrup by combining the sugar and water in a medium-size heavy-bottomed saucepan over medium-high heat. Add the lemon zest and juice and bring to a boil, stirring to dissolve the sugar. Boil for 2 minutes and remove from the heat.

Combine the dried fruits together in a large mixing bowl. Pour the simple syrup over them, toss to coat, and let steep for 5 minutes. Strain and reserve the syrup.

Cream the butter, sugar, and almond paste together in the bowl of an electric mixer fitted with a paddle at low speed, occasionally scraping down the sides of the bowl. Beat until the mixture is fluffy and smooth, about 2 minutes. Add the eggs one at a time, mixing in between each addition on low speed and scraping down the sides of the bowl as necessary. Add ½ cup of the Grand Marnier and mix to incorporate.

Combine the flour, baking powder, salt, cinnamon, and nutmeg in a medium-size mixing bowl and blend well. Add this mixture ½ cup at a time to the butter mixture with the mixer on low speed, each time mixing until smooth, about 2 minutes. Scrape down the sides of the bowl as necessary. The batter will be thick.

Add the warm fruit and all the nuts a little at a time, mixing well. Scrape down the sides of the bowl and the paddle.

Preheat the oven to 350°F.

Lightly grease twelve 1-pound loaf pans. Spoon about 1 cup of the batter into each pan. Bake until golden and the tops spring back when touched, about 45 minutes (rearranging them after 25 minutes if necessary to brown evenly).

Cool for 10 minutes in the pans. Remove cakes from the pans and cool completely on wire racks.

Wrap each cake in a layer of cheesecloth. Store in plastic storage bags until they are slightly stale, 3 to 4 days.

Combine the reserved simple syrup with the remaining ½ cup Grand Marnier and the bourbon. Without removing the cheesecloth, make tiny holes with a toothpick randomly on the top of each cake. Pour 2 tablespoons of the syrup over the top of each cake once every 2 to 3 days until all of the syrup is used. Let the cakes age for up to 3 weeks before eating.

WHISKEY SAUCE

MAKES ABOUT 3 CUPS

3 cups heavy cream
½ cup bourbon
½ cup granulated sugar
¼ cup plus 2 tablespoons cornstarch

Combine 2¾ cups of the cream with the bourbon and sugar in a medium-size nonstick saucepan over medium heat. Stir to dissolve the sugar.

In a small bowl, dissolve the cornstarch in the remaining ¼ cup cream. Add this to the cream-and-bourbon mixture and simmer stirring often, until the mixture thickens, 4 to 5 minutes. Remove from the heat and serve warm with the fruitcake.

The sauce may be stored, after it has cooled, in an airtight container for 24 hours. When ready to serve, warm over low heat.

BIG BOY COOKIES

MAKES ABOUT 2½ DOZEN

¾ pound (3 sticks) unsalted butter,
   at room temperature
1 cup plus 2 tablespoons
   granulated sugar
6 large egg yolks
1 teaspoon pure vanilla extract
2 cups plus 2 tablespoons bleached
   all-purpose flour
1 cup ground pecans
¾ teaspoon salt

Stocking Tip ■ Once the dough is removed from the refrigerator, work quickly so that it doesn't get soft.

Cream the butter and sugar in the bowl of an electric mixer fitted with a paddle on medium speed, scraping down the sides of the bowl as necessary. Cream the mixture until it is smooth and fluffy. Add the egg yolks one at a time, mixing in between each addition. Scrape down the sides of the bowl. Beat for 1 minute and add the vanilla.

Combine the flour, pecans, and salt in a medium-size mixing bowl and mix well. Add to the butter mixture and mix on low speed until it is fully incorporated. Increase the speed to medium and mix until the batter is thick and creamy, about 2 minutes. Scrape down the sides of the bowl and the paddle.

Generously dust a large sheet of parchment or waxed paper with flour. Spoon the dough down the center of the paper, fold the paper tightly over the dough, and roll into a cylinder about 3 inches in diameter and 12 to 14 inches long. Refrigerate for 8 hours.

Preheat the oven to 350°F.

Line a baking sheet with parchment or waxed paper.

Remove the dough from the refrigerator and peel away the paper. Using a sharp knife, cut the dough crosswise into ½-inch-thick slices. Place them on the baking sheet about 2 inches apart. Bake until lightly golden, about 20 minutes. Remove the cookies from the oven and let cool completely in the pan. Remove the cookies from the pan using a spatula or thin knife. Repeat the process until all of the dough is used.

Store in an airtight container for up to 2 weeks.

NEW ORLEANS

NEW YEAR'S EVE

DINNER

MY FRIEND MARCELLE CALLS

THE WEEK between Christmas and New Year's a lull between two storms. That is not to say that there's nothing going on, for there are always impromptu parties and get-togethers, but it's also the time to leisurely drink in all that comprises the holiday spirit.

She tells me that during the holidays of her childhood her parents would get up before dawn and make the three-hour journey by car to the city to view the decorations in the department stores and hotels, especially the display at the old Roosevelt Hotel, now The Fairmont. Every year the elegant block-long lobby of this grand old hotel was transformed into a fantasy of spun glass, snow-white smilax, glistening white bells, and multicolored lights. This annual holiday tradition that began in the mid-1940s continued until 1966 when, because of fire safety regulations, the management reluctantly discontinued the display.

But now, after an absence of thirty years, the display has returned. The canopy is now made of flame-retardant white batting and approximately 1,000 strands of cord and 30,000 lights. Gold papier-mâché cherubs, moons, stars, icicles, snowflakes, and giant metallic ornaments make the lobby look much as it did in former years.

I must take this opportunity to let you in on some New Orleans historic trivia. In The Fairmont Hotel is the Sazerac Bar. It is claimed that the world's first cocktail, the Sazerac, was first mixed in a French Quarter bar in New Orleans'

MENU

For 8 to 10 people

◆

Smoked Salmon Terrine with Christmas Caviar Sauce

Rye Bread Croutons

◆

Truffle Potato Soup with Truffle Mushroom Dumplings and Fried Parsley

◆

Mixed Green Salad with Popcorn Rock Shrimp

◆

Andouille-crusted Oysters with Spinach Coulis

Crawfish-stuffed Pork Chops with Crawfish Bordelaise Sauce

Caramelized Sweet Potatoes

◆

Banana Cream Pie with Caramel Drizzle and Chocolate Sauces

Chocolate Truffles

WINE PAIRINGS

I think this celebration dinner should start with a good sparkling wine, whether from California or Champagne. Sparkling wine is the perfect aperitif. It can be paired with dishes throughout the meal.

◆

SAUVIGNON BLANC
Sancerre, Pouilly-Fumé, New Zealand Sauvignon Blanc

Salmon and Sauvignon Blanc are perfect together. The citrus flavors of the wine complement the salmon, the acidity cutting through the richness of the fish.

◆

RHÔNE VARIETAL WHITE (CHÂTEAUNEUF-DU-PAPE BLANC, HERMITAGE BLANC):
Australia, California

Wines made from the Rhône varietals Marsanne and Rousanne, although not very common, can be very exciting when paired with certain dishes. At Emeril's we love the combination of truffles and Rhône whites. The wines are very floral with a slight earthiness. The aromas of the wine and truffles explode with this pairing.

RIESLING OR GEWÜRZTRAMINER
Germany, Alsace

The next two courses have very spicy components and require wines with a slight sweetness, but high acidity. A sweet wine will make the dish seem less spicy, and the wine will taste full of fruit and refreshing.

◆

SANGIOVESE: *Italy (Chianti, Brunello), California*

Many are familiar with Sangiovese from the wicker-basket Chiantis of the 1970s. However, much has changed. Good Sangiovese today is a deep, rich, full-of-cherry fruit wine with a very long finish. We have found it to be a great match with pork. The intense flavors combine very nicely.

◆

MUSCAT
California, France

Emeril's banana cream pie is very easy to pair with sweet white wine. My favorite is a good Muscat—rich, intense with lychee nuts, bananas, honey, and spice. The wine is very refreshing after a huge meal.

Exchange Alley in 1859. The name originated from a particular brand of imported cognac favored by New Orleanians then—it was Sazerac-de-Forge et fils. The Sazerac Bar moved from the French Quarter to the Central Business District. Then, in 1938, the Roosevelt Hotel created a new bar off the main lobby, commonly referred to as the "Main Bar." In 1949, the Roosevelt bought out the Sazerac Bar and obtained rights from the Sazerac Company, Inc., for the name of the bar and the rights to serve the Sazerac cocktail. The famed bar was also relocated next to the hotel on Baronne Street. The walls were embellished with murals that all paid tribute to the Sazerac, the royal libation of Rex, king of Mardi Gras. This was the sacrosanct bastion of males that members of the fair sex, who were banned from entering the bar save only on Mardi Gras, stormed September 26, 1949, and have been allowed ever since.

Whew! Now you know a great story to tell your friends.

Is it any wonder that New Orleans is known as a blowout celebration kind of city? Here in a metropolis that is referred to as the City That Care Forgot, anytime is a good time for a party, and especially on New Year's Eve. It's time to make merry, kick up one's heels, paint the town red, have a fling.

Out in the country, Marcelle says that New Year's Eve was, and still is, the time that adults, dressed to the nines, stepped out on the town, going from house to house, then ending up at an appointed night spot to toast in the New Year.

Children are sent off to *grandmère's* house for the night, where they anxiously await the arrival of *Le Petit Bonhomme Janvier,* the Little Man of January, who comes only when good little children are fast asleep. He leaves sacks, hung on the bedposts, filled with candy, crayons, oranges, and storybooks.

Marcelle recalls, too, that when her Tante Belle had trouble getting children to sleep, she would switch on the radio and tune it to WWL in New Orleans. The children gathered on quilts spread on the floor and huddled near the radio to listen to music "live from

the Blue Room," which, coincidentally, was housed in the Roosevelt Hotel. The Blue Room came into being on New Year's Eve 1935 and soon became known as America's premier nightclub. Sophie Tucker, Joe E. Lewis, Jimmy Durante, and Phil Harris all played the room. They were backed by equally big-name bands like Glenn Miller, the Dorsey Brothers, and Guy Lombardo. Marcelle and her siblings thought it was magical to be able to listen to the sounds of music that traveled the airways all the way from the big city to their little house in the country.

Every year, there are any number of shindigs to attend in New Orleans, and I'm usually working like crazy at the restaurant making sure that everyone's celebration goes off without a hitch.

But you can have your very own great party at your place with this menu that I've planned for you. Here's what I'd do. Set the table with lots of splashy colors, glitter, and glitzy party favors. Ice down Champagne, lots of it. After the guests arrive, settle in for a leisurely, jolly feast while you and your guests wait for the midnight hour.

And what a feast it is. Begin with Smoked Salmon Terrine with Christmas Caviar Sauce. It's marvelous! Then

SHOPPING LIST

FLOUR, LEAVENERS, AND OTHER BAKING AISLE INGREDIENTS

Bleached all-purpose flour *(4 cups, about 1⅓ pounds)*
Masa harina flour *(½ cup)*
Rye flour *(2 cups)*
Yellow cornmeal *(½ cup)*
Cornstarch *(¾ cup)*
Dry yeast *(one ¼-ounce envelope)*
Confectioners' sugar *(2 tablespoons)*
Granulated sugar *(1¾ pounds)*
Firmly packed light brown sugar *(1 cup)*
Graham cracker crumbs *(3 cups)*
Semisweet chocolate *(about 2 pounds)*
Dipping chocolate *(about 2 pounds)*
Unsweetened cocoa powder *(½ cup)*
Chocolate block *(½ pound)*
Steen's 100% Pure Cane Syrup *(1 cup)*
Dark molasses *(½ cup)*
Dark corn syrup *(½ cup)*
Semisweet chocolate chips *(½ pound)*

SPICES, DRIED HERBS, AND EXTRACTS

Grated nutmeg *(⅛ teaspoon)*
Ground cloves *(¼ teaspoon)*
Ground allspice *(⅛ teaspoon)*
Ground cinnamon *(½ teaspoon)*
Salt *(about ½ cup)*

Black peppercorns *(3 teaspoons)*
Black pepper *(about 3½ teaspoons)*
Cayenne *(about 4½ teaspoons)*
White pepper *(about ½ teaspoon)*
Dry mustard *(1 teaspoon)*
Sweet paprika *(2½ tablespoons)*
Garlic powder *(2 tablespoons)*
Onion powder *(1 tablespoon)*
Bay leaves *(14)*
Basil *(1 teaspoon)*
Oregano *(1 tablespoon plus 1 teaspoon)*
Tarragon *(1 teaspoon)*
Thyme *(1 tablespoon)*
Vanilla bean *(1)*
Pure vanilla extract *(¾ teaspoon)*

OILS

Olive oil *(about ½ cup)*
Vegetable oil *(2½ quarts)*
White truffle oil *(2 tablespoons plus ½ teaspoon)*
Extra virgin olive oil *(4½ cups)*

PRODUCE

Assorted mixed baby salad greens *(10 cups)*
Spinach *(one 10-ounce bag)*
Fresh plum tomatoes *(4)*
Red bell peppers *(2 medium-size, 1 small)*
Yellow bell pepper *(1 small)*
Fresh cayenne pepper *(¼ pound)*
Carrots *(about ½ pound)*
Celery *(1 large head)*

Exotic mushrooms (*1/2 pound*)

Chives (*1 tablespoon*)

Parsley (*8 sprigs*)

Thyme (*10 sprigs*)

Tarragon (*5 sprigs*)

Garlic (*5 heads*)

Green onions (*called scallions everywhere but in Louisiana, 2 small bunches*)

Red onion (*1*)

Yellow onions (*10 medium-size*)

Shallots (*10 large*)

Baking potatoes (*1 1/2 pounds*)

Sweet potatoes (*2 large, about 2 pounds*)

Bananas (*3 1/4 pounds*)

Lemons (*2 large or 3 medium-size*)

DAIRY

Large eggs (*9*)

Half-and-half (*1 cup*)

Heavy cream (*2 1/2 quarts*)

Sour cream (*1 1/4 cups*)

Unsalted butter (*3 1/2 sticks*)

Cream cheese (*12 ounces*)

Parmigiano-Reggiano cheese (*about 1/4 pound*)

CONDIMENTS AND CANNED GOODS

Caviar (*about 3 1/2 tablespoons*)

Salmon roe (*1 1/2 teaspoons*)

Wasabi-injected roe (*2 tablespoons*)

Creole or whole-grain mustard (*1 tablespoon*)

Tabasco sauce (*1/4 teaspoon*)

Tomato paste (*1/4 cup*)

FISH AND SEAFOOD COUNTER

Rock shrimp (*1 pound*)

Shucked oysters (*32*)

Crawfish tail meat, peeled (*1 1/2 pounds*)

Smoked salmon (*1 pound*)

MEAT DEPARTMENT

Andouille or kielbasa sausage (*1/4 pound*)

Raw chicken bones (*4 pounds*)

Duck carcasses (*4 pounds*)

Double-cut pork loin chops (*8 to 10, each 14 to 16 ounces*)

LIQUOR AND WINE

Brandy (*2 teaspoons*)

Dry red wine (*1 1/2 cups*)

Grand Marnier or other orange-flavored liqueur (*1/2 cup*)

Herbsaint or other anise-flavored liqueur (*1/4 cup*)

MISCELLANEOUS

Dried fine white bread crumbs (*1 3/4 cups*)

Whole truffles (*2*)

Won ton wrappers (*20*)

Parchment or waxed paper

follow with a creamy potato soup dolled up with truffles and mushroom dumplings.

Refresh your mouth with a mixed green salad tossed with crispy-fried rock shrimp. The rest of the meal includes a personal favorite, oysters encrusted with our Louisiana sausage, andouille, and, the *pièce de resistance,* double-cut pork chops stuffed with crawfish, accompanied by Caramelized Sweet Potatoes. The pork chops are big, but don't be intimidated. I've witnessed elegantly dressed ladies tear into them!

For dessert, serve this incredible Banana Cream Pie (which we serve at Emeril's), drizzled with chocolate sauce as well as caramel sauce. Pass around the chocolate truffles for an extra sweet treat.

Sip some more bubbly and have a happy, happy New Year!

SMOKED SALMON TERRINE WITH CHRISTMAS CAVIAR SAUCE

1 pound smoked salmon, thinly sliced
12 ounces cream cheese (1½ cups),
  at room temperature
½ teaspoon chopped garlic
1 teaspoon minced yellow onion
2 teaspoons finely chopped fresh parsley
  leaves
¼ cup (½ stick) unsalted butter
2 teaspoons brandy
1 tablespoon fresh lemon juice
2 tablespoons heavy cream
½ recipe Christmas Caviar Sauce
  (page 58)

FOR GARNISH
Caviar
Finely chopped red onions
Minced fresh parsley leaves
Rye Bread Croutons (page 77)

Stocking Tip ■ Often heralded as the king of smoked fish, salmon is usually served as an appetizer in paper-thin slices. The salmon used here was cut into large slices. However, if the salmon is cut into smaller slices, you may need to use more of them to cover the bottom of the bowl and the top of the terrine. The weight needed remains the same.

Line a 4-cup glass bowl with plastic wrap, with the wrap overhanging the sides of the bowl about 2 inches. Cover the bottom of the bowl with 1 to 2 slices of the salmon. Line the sides of the bowl with 5 to 6 slices of the salmon, allowing the slices to overlap the bowl by about ¼ inch. Reserve 1 to 2 slices of the salmon for the top of the terrine. Set aside.

Purée the cream cheese in a food processor until smooth. Add the remaining salmon and process until the mixture is smooth, about 1 minute. Scrape down the sides of the bowl. Add the garlic, onion, parsley, butter, brandy, lemon juice, and cream and process until the mixture is smooth again, another minute.

Spoon the mixture into the salmon-lined bowl. Place the reserved salmon slices on top of the mixture. Fold the overlapping slices of salmon toward the center. Fold the plastic wrap over the top of the terrine and cover tightly. Refrigerate for 12 hours or up to 3 days.

Remove the terrine from the refrigerator and carefully open the plastic wrap. Invert it onto a serving platter and remove the plastic wrap. Cut the terrine into small wedges.

To serve, spread a tablespoon of the caviar sauce on the bottom of a serving plate. Top with a wedge of terrine and serve with the garnishes.

TRUFFLE POTATO SOUP WITH TRUFFLE MUSHROOM DUMPLINGS AND FRIED PARSLEY

MAKES ABOUT 10 SERVINGS

¼ cup (½ stick) unsalted butter
1¼ pounds yellow onions, thinly sliced
 (about 4 cups)
3 ribs celery, chopped (about 1 cup)
1 teaspoon salt
¼ teaspoon cayenne
⅛ teaspoon freshly ground black pepper
¼ pound assorted exotic mushrooms,
 such as shiitakes, chanterelles, and
 oysters, wiped clean and chopped
 (about 1½ cups)
4 bay leaves
3 tablespoons chopped garlic
10 cups Chicken Stock (page 30)
1½ pounds baking potatoes, peeled and
 diced (about 4 cups)
¼ cup heavy cream
2 tablespoons white truffle oil
Truffle Mushroom Dumplings
 (page 76)
Fried Parsley (page 76)
Shaved black truffles for garnish
 (optional)

Melt the butter in a 6-quart stock-pot over medium-high heat. Add the onions, celery, salt, cayenne, and black pepper and cook, stirring, until the vegetables are very soft and lightly golden, about 8 minutes. Add the mushrooms, bay leaves, and garlic and cook, stirring, for 2 minutes. Add the stock and potatoes and bring the mix-ture to a boil. Reduce the heat to medium and simmer, uncovered, un-til the potatoes are very soft and the mixture is thick and creamy, about 1 hour and 15 minutes.

Remove the soup from the heat. Discard the bay leaves. With a hand-held emersion blender, purée the soup until smooth. Slowly add the cream and truffle oil. Stir gently to blend.

Ladle the soup into individual bowls, add two dumplings to each bowl, and top with the fried parsley and shavings of truffle, if you wish.

TRUFFLE MUSHROOM DUMPLINGS

¼ cup (½ stick) unsalted butter
¼ pound assorted exotic mushrooms,
  such as shiitakes, chanterelles, and
  oysters, wiped clean and chopped
  (about 1½ cups)
2 tablespoons minced shallots
1 tablespoon chopped garlic
¾ teaspoon salt plus a pinch
⅛ teaspoon freshly ground
  black pepper
¼ cup heavy cream
½ teaspoon white truffle oil
  (optional)
8 cups water
20 won ton wrappers

Stocking Tip ■ Won ton wrappers are paper-thin sheets of dough made from flour, eggs, and salt. They can be purchased prepackaged in some supermarkets in the produce or refrigerated section and in most Chinese markets. The wrappers usually come in both squares and circles. We used the squares.

Melt the butter in a medium-size sauté pan over medium heat. Add the mushrooms and cook, stirring, for 2 minutes. Add the shallots, garlic, ¼ teaspoon of the salt, and the black pepper and cook another 2 minutes, stirring occasionally. Add the cream and truffle oil if using. Simmer the mixture for 30 seconds. Remove from the heat and let cool completely.

Put the water and ½ teaspoon of the salt in a large saucepan and bring to a boil.

Meanwhile, spoon 1½ teaspoons of the mushroom mixture in the center of each won ton wrapper. Lightly brush the edges with water. Fold one corner to the opposite corner to form a triangle. Crimp the edges and seal.

Poach the won tons, several at a time, in the boiling water until soft and tender, about 3 minutes. Remove them from the water with a slotted spoon and drain on paper towels. Season with the pinch of salt.

FRIED PARSLEY

2 cups vegetable oil for deep frying
1 bunch parsley sprigs, washed
  and patted dry
Salt

Heat the oil in a large pot or electric fryer to 360°F.

Drop the parsley into the hot oil for about 30 seconds. Be careful, as the oil may splatter. Remove with a slotted spoon and drain on paper towels. Sprinkle with salt to taste.

RYE BREAD CROUTONS

MAKES 1 LOAF

1 envelope (¼ ounce) dry yeast
1¼ cups warm water (about 110°F)
2 tablespoons granulated sugar
2 tablespoons unsalted butter
1 large egg
3 cups bleached all-purpose flour
2 cups rye flour
1 tablespoon salt
1 teaspoon vegetable oil

Stocking Tip ■ Rye flour contains fewer gluten-forming proteins than all-purpose or whole-wheat flour. It's also heavier and darker than other flours, which makes it perfect for this delightful dense bread. It's available in some supermarkets or specialty food shops.

Combine the yeast, water, sugar, and butter in the bowl of an electric mixer fitted with a dough hook. Beat for 1 minute on low speed to dissolve the yeast. Let sit until the mixture begins to foam. If it doesn't foam, the yeast is no longer active and must be replaced. Add the egg and beat at low speed for 1 minute. Add both flours and the salt. Beat at low speed until the flour is fully incorporated, about 1 minute. Then beat at medium speed until the mixture forms a ball, leaves the sides of the bowl, and climbs up the dough hook.

Remove the dough from the bowl. Using your hands, form the dough into a smooth ball. Lightly grease a bowl with the oil. Place the dough in the bowl and turn to oil all sides. Cover with plastic wrap and set aside in a warm, draft-free place until doubled in size, about 2 hours.

Punch the dough down and put into a lightly greased 9¼ × 5¼ × 2¾-inch loaf pan. Cover it with plastic wrap and set aside in a warm, draft-free place until almost doubled in size, about an hour.

Preheat the oven to 350°F.

Bake until golden brown, about 45 minutes. Remove from the oven and let stand for about 5 minutes. Turn onto a wire rack and cool. Cut into ¼-inch-thick slices and remove the crusts. Cut each slice diagonally into two triangles. Place them on a baking sheet and lightly toast in the oven.

MIXED GREEN SALAD WITH POPCORN ROCK SHRIMP

MAKES 10 SERVINGS

2 heads garlic
2 medium-size red bell peppers
1½ teaspoons salt
⅛ teaspoon freshly ground white pepper
2 tablespoons olive oil
1 large egg
1 tablespoon Creole or whole-grain
   mustard
1 tablespoon fresh lemon juice
1 cup Hot Pepper Oil (page 79)
1 cup vegetable oil
½ cup heavy cream
¼ teaspoon Tabasco sauce
5 teaspoons Creole Seasoning
   (page 30)
1 pound rock shrimp, peeled
½ cup yellow cornmeal
½ cup masa harina flour
4 cups vegetable oil for deep frying
10 cups mixed baby salad greens, such
   as romaine, frisée, red oak leaf, and
   radicchio, washed and patted dry
½ cup freshly grated Parmigiano-
   Reggiano cheese
⅛ teaspoon freshly ground
   black pepper

Stocking Tips ■ An alternative way to serve this is to omit the greens and serve the shrimp with a bowl of the dressing on a tray as a passed appetizer. Any remaining dressing can be spread on sandwiches. ■ In most parts of the country—other than in Florida, where they are caught locally—these delicious little shrimp are sold without their heads and already peeled because the shells are tough and hard to remove. Although rock shrimp are small, they have a firm texture and a lobsterlike flavor. If they are unavailable in your area, substitute any local fresh or frozen shrimp, preferably 71/90 count per pound.

Preheat the oven to 400°F.

Line a baking sheet with parchment or waxed paper.

Cut about ¼ inch off the tops of the garlic heads. Combine the garlic, bell peppers, ¼ teaspoon of the salt, the white pepper, and olive oil in a medium-size mixing bowl and toss to coat. Place the mixture on the baking sheet and roast until the garlic is tender and peppers soft, about 40 minutes.

Separate the garlic and the peppers. Put the peppers in a small mixing bowl, cover the bowl with plastic wrap, and let cool for 20 minutes.

Cool the garlic for about 10 minutes. Extract the flesh by squeezing each clove with your thumb and index finger.

Peel the skin off the peppers and remove their seeds.

Put the egg, mustard, lemon juice, peppers, and garlic in a food processor or blender and purée for 30 seconds. With the machine running, slowly pour the hot pepper oil and vegetable oil in through the feed tube. The mixture will be slightly thick and creamy. Add an-

other ¼ teaspoon salt and pulse once or twice to blend. Set aside.

Combine the cream, Tabasco, ½ teaspoon of the salt, and 1 teaspoon of the Creole seasoning in a medium-size mixing bowl. Add the shrimp and toss to mix. Cover tightly with plastic wrap and let sit for 30 minutes in the refrigerator. Drain.

In a small mixing bowl, combine the cornmeal, masa harina, and 2 teaspoons of the Creole seasoning. Dredge the shrimp in the cornmeal mixture, coating them evenly and tapping off any excess.

Heat the frying oil in a deep pot or an electric deep-fryer to 360°F. Fry the shrimp 4 to 5 at a time, until golden brown, about 2 minutes. Drain on paper towels. When they're all fried, season them with the remaining 2 teaspoons Creole seasoning.

Toss the mixed greens with ½ cup of the garlic dressing, the remaining ½ teaspoon salt, the cheese, and black pepper. Mound the greens in the center of a platter. Sprinkle the shrimp over the greens. Serve immediately.

Hot Pepper Oil

MAKES ABOUT 1 QUART

6 cloves garlic, peeled and thinly sliced
    lengthwise
1 cup distilled white vinegar
4½ cups extra virgin olive oil
¼ pound fresh cayenne peppers
    (about 60)
½ teaspoon cayenne
2 teaspoons salt

Combine the garlic and vinegar in a small bowl and let sit for 24 hours. Drain off the vinegar.

Combine the garlic, olive oil, whole peppers, cayenne, and salt in a 2-quart saucepan over medium heat. Simmer for 15 minutes, stirring occasionally. Remove from the heat and let steep for 45 minutes.

Pour half of the oil into a food processor with half of the peppers and half of the garlic slices and process until smooth, about 20 seconds.

Sterilize a quart-size bottle or jar. Place the remaining peppers and garlic in the container. Pour in the pureed mixture and the remaining oil. Cool and secure with an airtight lid. Store in the refrigerator for 2 weeks before using. Will keep for 1 month in the refrigerator.

ANDOUILLE-CRUSTED OYSTERS WITH SPINACH COULIS

MAKES 8 SERVINGS

1 tablespoon olive oil
¼ pound andouille or kielbasa sausage,
  finely chopped (about ¾ cup)
2 teaspoons chopped garlic
1 tablespoon chopped shallots
1¼ cups dried fine white bread crumbs
5 teaspoons Creole Seasoning
  (page 30)
1 cup bleached all-purpose flour
1 large egg, beaten
⅓ cup half-and-half
32 shucked oysters, drained well
1 cup vegetable oil
1 recipe Spinach Coulis (page 85)

Stocking Tip ■ Andouille is a smoked sausage made with pork and seasoned with garlic, salt, and hot peppers. It is similar to the Polish sausage kielbasa, which can be used as a substitute.

Heat the olive oil in a 10-inch sauté pan over high heat. Add the sausage and brown it, cooking 2 to 3 minutes. Add the garlic and shallots and cook, stirring, until slightly soft, about 1 minute.

Remove from the heat and let cool for about 5 minutes.

In a small bowl, combine the sausage with the bread crumbs and 2 teaspoons of the Creole seasoning. Mix well.

In a shallow bowl, combine the flour and 2 teaspoons of the Creole seasoning. Mix well.

In another small bowl, blend the egg, half-and-half, and the remaining teaspoon Creole seasoning.

Dredge the oysters in the flour, coating evenly and tapping off any excess. Dip the oysters in the egg mixture, then dredge them in the bread crumb-and-sausage mixture, coating evenly. Heat the oil in a large skillet over medium-high heat. When the oil is hot but not smoking, lay about half of the oysters in the skillet. Panfry until browned, about 2 minutes, then turn them over and fry another 2 minutes. Drain on paper towels. Repeat the frying process with the remaining oysters.

To serve, spread ¼ cup of the spinach coulis in the center of each of eight dinner plates and place four oysters on top of the coulis. Serve immediately.

CRAWFISH-STUFFED PORK CHOPS WITH CRAWFISH BORDELAISE SAUCE

MAKES 8 TO 10 SERVINGS

2 tablespoons olive oil
½ cup chopped yellow onions
2 tablespoons seeded and finely chopped
    red bell pepper
2 tablespoons seeded and finely chopped
    yellow bell pepper
2 teaspoons salt
½ teaspoon cayenne
1 pound peeled crawfish tails
¼ cup chopped green onions (scallions),
    green parts only
1 tablespoon chopped garlic
2 tablespoons chopped fresh parsley
    leaves
1 large egg
½ cup dried fine white bread crumbs
¼ cup freshly grated Parmigiano-
    Reggiano cheese
8 to 10 double-cut pork loin chops,
    2½ to 3 inches thick, 14 to 16
    ounces each
4 to 5 teaspoons Creole Seasoning
    (page 30)
½ cup vegetable oil
Crawfish Bordelaise Sauce (page 84)

Stocking Tip ■ You may have to ask your butcher to custom-cut these chops.

Preheat the oven to 400°F.

Heat the olive oil over medium heat in a medium-size sauté pan and add the onions, bell peppers, salt, and cayenne. Cook for 2 minutes, stirring occasionally. Add the crawfish tails and cook, stirring, for 2 minutes. Add the green onions, garlic, and parsley and cook, stirring, for 1 minute.

Pour the mixture into a medium-size mixing bowl and let cool for about 2 minutes. Add the egg, bread crumbs, and cheese and mix well. Set aside.

Using a sharp knife, cut a pocket into the side of each pork chop about 1¼ inches deep and 3 inches long. Season each chop, on the outside and in the pocket, with about ½ teaspoon of the Creole seasoning. Stuff each chop with ¼ cup of the crawfish mixture. Press the filling firmly into the pockets.

Heat ¼ cup of the vegetable oil in each of two large skillets over medium-high heat. Sear the chops for 6 minutes on the first side, being careful not to char them. The color should be a little darker than golden. Turn them over and sear the other side for 4 minutes.

Line a baking sheet with parchment or waxed paper and set the chops on the paper. Roast about 15 minutes for medium (145° to 150°F on an instant meat thermometer). Remove from the oven and let stand about 5 minutes before serving with the bordelaise sauce poured over each chop.

CRAWFISH BORDELAISE SAUCE

1 teaspoon olive oil
¼ cup chopped yellow onions
½ pound peeled crawfish tails
½ teaspoon salt
⅛ teaspoon cayenne
2 tablespoons minced shallots
2 teaspoons chopped garlic
½ cup chopped, peeled, and seeded
    fresh or canned Italian plum
    tomatoes
½ cup dry red wine
1 cup Duck Stock (page 57)
1 tablespoon finely chopped fresh
    parsley leaves
2 tablespoons chopped green onions
    (scallions), green parts only
1 tablespoon unsalted butter

Heat the oil in a sauté pan over medium heat. Add the onions and cook, stirring, for 1 minute. Add the crawfish tails, salt, and cayenne and cook, stirring for 2 minutes. Add the shallots, garlic, and tomatoes and cook, stirring for 2 minutes. Add the wine and simmer for 4 minutes. Add the stock, parsley, and green onions and simmer until slightly thick, about another 5 minutes. Add the butter and stir to combine, about 20 seconds.

Serve warm with the pork chops.

CARAMELIZED SWEET POTATOES

MAKES 10 SERVINGS

1 tablespoon unsalted butter
2 large sweet potatoes (about
   2 pounds), washed, ends removed,
   and cut into 1-inch dice
½ cup Spiced Glaze (page 58)

Preheat the oven to 400°F.

Grease a 2-quart glass rectangular baking dish with the butter.

Toss the sweet potatoes in a large mixing bowl with the glaze to coat evenly. Pour them into the prepared pan and roast until fork-tender, about 1 hour. Serve warm.

SPINACH COULIS

MAKES 2 CUPS

1 tablespoon unsalted butter
¼ cup chopped shallots
¼ cup Herbsaint or other anise-
   flavored liqueur
¼ cup chopped green onions
   (scallions), green parts only
1 tablespoon chopped fresh parsley
   leaves
One 10-ounce bag fresh spinach,
   thoroughly washed and trimmed of
   tough stems
¾ cup heavy cream
½ teaspoon salt
⅛ teaspoon freshly ground white
   pepper

Heat the butter in a 10-inch sauté pan over medium heat. Add the shallots and cook, stirring, until soft and lightly golden, about 2 minutes. Carefully add the Herbsaint so that it does not flame. Add the green onions, parsley, and spinach and cook until the spinach is slightly wilted, about 1 minute. Add the cream and simmer for 2 minutes, stirring occasionally.

Pour the mixture into a food processor or blender and process until the mixture is smooth, about 1 minute. Add the salt and pepper and pulse two or three times to blend, and serve immediately.

BANANA CREAM PIE

ONE 9-INCH PIE; 8 TO 10 SERVINGS

5 large egg yolks
¾ cup cornstarch
3 to 3½ cups heavy cream
2 cups granulated sugar
1 vanilla bean, split and scraped
3 cups graham cracker crumbs
½ ripe banana, mashed
¼ pound (1 stick) unsalted butter,
    melted
3 pounds bananas, cut crosswise
    into ½-inch-thick slices
1 recipe Caramel Drizzle Sauce
    (page 88)
1 recipe Chocolate Sauce (page 88)
2 cups heavy cream whipped to
    stiff peaks with ½ teaspoon pure
    vanilla extract and 2 teaspoons
    granulated sugar
Shaved chocolate
Confectioners' sugar

Stocking Tips ■ Vanilla beans are long and thin. To get the essence of the bean, it must be split, then scraped to remove the resinous, pasty insides. Lay the bean on a flat surface with its seam facing up. Using a sharp knife, place the point in the seam at the center and split to one end. Place the point back at the center and split it to the other end. Use the blade of the knife to scrape the pasty seeds out. ■ To make shaved chocolate, chill a block of chocolate. Using a vegetable peeler, shave the sides of the block.

Combine the egg yolks, cornstarch, and 1 cup of the heavy cream in a small bowl and whisk to blend well. Set aside.

Combine the remaining 2 cups cream, 1½ cups of the sugar, and the vanilla bean in a large heavy-bottomed saucepan over medium heat. Whisk to dissolve the sugar and bring it to a gentle boil, about 10 minutes. Slowly add the egg yolk mixture, whisking constantly until it thickens, about 5 minutes. Be forewarned: the mixture will break. Don't be alarmed. Pour it into a glass bowl. Press a piece of plastic wrap down over the surface of the mixture to prevent a skin from forming. Let cool completely at room temperature.

When cooled, remove the vanilla bean and pour the mixture into the bowl of an electric mixer fitted with a wire whip. Beat at medium speed to combine the mixture. If it will not combine, warm another ½ cup heavy cream and slowly add it to the mixture. Whip until you have a thick and creamy custard.

Preheat the oven to 350°F.

Combine the graham cracker crumbs, the remaining ½ cup sugar, and the mashed banana in a large mixing bowl. Thoroughly mix together. Add the butter and mix well. Press the mixture into a 9-inch pie pan and bake until browned, about 25 minutes. Let cool for about 10 minutes.

continued

To assemble, spread about ½ cup of the custard on the bottom of the crust. Arrange about a third of the banana slices, crowding them close together, over the custard. Next, spread 1 cup of the custard over the bananas. Arrange another third of the banana slices close together over the custard. Top with 1 cup custard and the remaining banana slices. Top with the remaining custard, covering the bananas completely to prevent them from turning brown.

Cover with plastic wrap and chill for at least 4 hours.

To serve, cut the pie into wedges and drizzle on the caramel sauce and chocolate sauce. Top with the whipped cream and shaved chocolate. Sprinkle with confectioners' sugar.

CARAMEL DRIZZLE SAUCE

MAKES ABOUT ¾ CUP

1 cup granulated sugar
¼ cup water
1 cup heavy cream

In a small, heavy-bottomed saucepan, combine the sugar and water and bring the mixture to a boil, stirring often. Cook, stirring occasionally, until the mixture is a deep caramel color and has the consistency of a thin syrup, 10 to 15 minutes. Remove from the heat. Stir in the cream, return the saucepan to high heat, and boil the sauce until it regains the consistency of a thick syrup, about 2 minutes. Cool.

The sauce can be refrigerated until ready to use. Allow it to reach room temperature before drizzling it over the pie.

CHOCOLATE SAUCE

MAKES ABOUT 1½ CUPS

¾ cup half-and-half
1 tablespoon unsalted butter
½ pound semisweet chocolate chips
¼ teaspoon pure vanilla extract

Combine the half-and-half and butter in a small heavy-bottomed saucepan over medium heat. Heat the mixture until a thin paperlike skin appears on the top. Do not boil. Add the chocolate and vanilla and stir until the chocolate melts and the mixture is smooth.

Remove from the heat and let cool.

The sauce can be kept refrigerated for several days, but it must be returned to room temperature before serving.

CHOCOLATE TRUFFLES

ABOUT 80 TRUFFLES

2 cups heavy cream
2 pounds semisweet chocolate, chopped
2 tablespoons unsalted butter
½ cup Grand Marnier or other orange-
    flavored liqueur (optional)
½ cup unsweetened cocoa powder
½ cup granulated sugar

In a large, heavy-bottomed sauce-pan, heat the cream over medium heat until it just begins to simmer, about 5 minutes. Add the chocolate. With a wooden spoon, stir until the chocolate melts and the mixture is smooth, about 5 minutes. Add the butter and stir to melt completely.

If you wish to flavor the mixture, add the Grand Marnier at this point.

Line a baking pan with parchment or waxed paper. Pour the chocolate into the pan, spreading it evenly with a wooden spoon. Let it cool completely, then refrigerate until it sets.

Remove the chocolate from the parchment paper, break it into pieces, and put it in the bowl of an electric mixer fitted with a wire whisk. Beat at low speed for 1 minute, then increase the speed to medium and beat until it is creamy and smooth, 2 to 3 minutes.

Stocking Tip ■ To make the piping of the truffles easier and less messy, make a "bullet." Take a sheet of plastic wrap about 2 feet square and place it on your work surface. Put the chocolate mixture in the center of the wrap. Fold the plastic wrap over the mixture, molding it firmly into a log or bullet. Secure each end by twisting the wrap tightly. Snip off one end and slide it into a pastry bag, then proceed as usual.

Transfer the mixture to a pastry bag without a tip. Pipe out ½-ounce truffles, each about the size of a walnut, onto a sheet of parchment or waxed paper.

Combine the cocoa powder and sugar in a shallow bowl. Using two forks, roll the truffles in the mixture, coating them evenly. Transfer to a sheet of parchment paper and leave to harden at room temperature or refrigerate. Store the truffles between layers of parchment paper in an airtight container. Will keep up to 1 week.

VARIATION: An alternative is to dip the truffles in melted chocolate. After piping out the truffles, refrigerate for at least 4 hours. Use dipping chocolate (called couverture), which is available in bittersweet, semisweet, white, or milk chocolate varieties in specialty food shops. It melts easily and smoothly. If you plan to dip all of the truffles, you will need about 2 pounds of chocolate, but if you want to do only two or three dozen, you will need about a pound. Work in a cool, dry room. Melt the chocolate in a stainless-steel bowl set over simmering water. Use a four-prong fork to dip, then tip the truffles onto a sheet of parchment paper by turning the fork upside down. Avoid touching the dipped candies while they set. Chocolate is shinier if allowed to cool at room temperature. Refrigerate the candies only if the chocolate has not set after 15 minutes. After they set, put them in paper candy cups and store between sheets of parchment paper.

NEW YEAR'S DAY
SUPPER
FAMILY STYLE

IN THE OLD DAYS, NEW YEAR'S

DAY RATHER than Christmas was the time for receiving impor-

tant gifts. After the exchanging of presents, families set out to visit

close relatives. These calls were somewhat formal and brief, as families

had to return to their homes to receive callers who came later in the day.

Refreshments included wine, brandy, cordials, and liqueurs accompanied by plates of cakes, candies, and pralines. By late in the afternoon, after all the guests had departed, the family settled down to a grand dinner. There might have been raw oysters on the half shell, followed by a dark, thick turtle soup. The main dish might include both a large roasted hen and baked ducks. An array of seasonal vegetables was offered. Dessert was usually an elegant cake served with demitasse cups of strong, dark coffee.

MENU

For 10 people

◆

Jiffy Pop Firecracker Shrimp
Spicy Crab Cakes with
Fried Quail Eggs
Roasted Vegetable Pecan Relish
Creole Meunière Sauce

◆

Oyster and Parsley Chowder with
Parmesan Tuiles

◆

Caramelized Roasted Skillet Duck
with Steen's Duck Marinade
Caramelized Andouille Spoon Bread
Stewed Black-eyed Peas
Collard and Mustard Greens in
Ham Hock Gravy
Jalapeño and Cheese Biscuits

◆

Assorted Cheese Plate
Chocolate Bread Pudding with
Spiced Cream

While many old Creole families continue this tradition, I, a relative newcomer to The Crescent City, have my own style of celebration for the first day of the New Year.

New Year's Day is chill-out day for me. It's a day for enjoying the football games, visiting with friends, and ending with a leisurely supper. When I'm in charge of the meal, this is a menu that my friends enjoy—maybe yours will, too.

I created Jiffy Pop Firecracker Shrimp

WINE PAIRINGS

After the New Year's Eve celebration, you might not want sparkling wine. Beer will pair perfectly with the firecracker shrimp.

◆

PINOT GRIS / GRIGIO
Oregon, Alsace, Italy
Pinot Gris and Pinot Grigio are the same varietal. The high acidity and natural sweetness of the varietal make it very flexible. It has a fresh apple-lemon-lime flavor that will complement the crab cakes nicely.

◆

PINOT NOIR
Burgundy, California, Oregon
I love Pinot Noir. No other varietal is as aromatically pleasing, and Pinot Noir can be served with so many dishes. Duck is a natural complement. Whenever you have a question about what wine to serve, Pinot Noir is a great choice.

◆

TAWNY PORT
ten to twelve years old
Tawny port has been aged in wood for an extended period of time, usually ten or twenty years. The flavors are more subtle than those of ruby port. Coffee, caramel, and spice dominate this palate. It's ideal to serve with chocolate.

just for this occasion. It's a hoot to prepare and a holler to serve. The shrimp and popcorn are cooked in a tightly covered skillet. The sound and aroma of the popcorn popping puts everybody in just the right mood.

The Spicy Crab Cakes with Fried Quail Eggs served with a rich Cre-

ole Meunière Sauce is mighty good for the body and soul. When I can, I get dainty (Marcelle calls them precious) quail eggs from our local farms. This dish will set you right if you have a heavy head from the night before.

Follow the crab cakes with steaming hot Oyster and Parsley Chowder to get your gastric juices flowing. Then, it's a must in the South, especially in New Orleans, to eat black-eyed peas to bring you good luck and greens to bring you good fortune. The Caramelized Roasted Skillet Duck is *sooo* good you'll end up sucking on the bones. The Caramelized Andouille Spoon Bread and the Jalapeño and Cheese Biscuits are both stick-to-your-ribs food, my kind of sustenance.

You might want to take a breather before you chow down on the rich Chocolate Bread Pudding with Spiced Cream. I suggest that you make an extra pudding for you to enjoy alone after all your guests leave. I do. Go ahead, you deserve it!

There, you're set for the New Year. May it be a spectacular one!

SHOPPING LIST

FLOUR, LEAVENERS, AND OTHER BAKING AISLE INGREDIENTS

Bleached all-purpose flour
(1 pound plus 1½ cups)
Yellow cornmeal (1½ cups)
Baking powder (1½ tablespoons)
Granulated sugar (¼ cup)
Firmly packed light brown sugar (1 cup)
Steen's 100% Pure Cane Syrup (2 cups)
Dark molasses (½ cup)
Pecan halves (1 cup)
Semisweet chocolate chips (3 cups)

SPICES, DRIED HERBS, AND EXTRACTS

Salt (about 7½ tablespoons)
Kosher salt (¼ cup)
Black peppercorns (4 teaspoons)
Black pepper (about 4 teaspoons)
White pepper (½ teaspoon plus a pinch)
Cayenne (about 2½ tablespoons)
Sweet paprika (2½ tablespoons)
Garlic powder (2 tablespoons)
Onion powder (1 tablespoon)
Basil (2 teaspoons)
Oregano (1 tablespoon plus 2 teaspoons)
Tarragon (2 teaspoons)
Thyme (1 tablespoon)
Bay leaves (24)
Ground cinnamon (2 teaspoons)
Grated nutmeg (¼ teaspoon plus ⅛ teaspoon)
Pure vanilla extract (1 teaspoon)

OILS AND VINEGARS

Extra virgin olive oil (4½ cups)
Olive oil (2 tablespoons)
Sesame oil (2 tablespoons)
Vegetable oil (about 3 cups)
Vegetable shortening (1 cup plus 1 teaspoon)
Balsamic vinegar (¼ cup)

PRODUCE

Eggplant (1 large, about ½ pound)
Green bell pepper (1 small)
Red bell pepper (1 small)
Yellow bell pepper (1 small)
Fresh cayenne peppers (¼ pound, about 60)
Fresh jalapeños (2)
Collard greens (2¼ pounds)
Mustard greens (2¼ pounds)
Yellow squash (1 large, about ½ pound)
Zucchini (1 large, about ½ pound)
Carrots (about 2 pounds)
Celery (about 12 ribs or 2 large heads)
Fresh ginger (one 2-inch piece)
Parsley (2 bunches)
Fresh thyme (5 sprigs)
Garlic (5 heads)
Green onions (scallions everywhere
else but in Louisiana, 1 bunch)
Yellow onions (about 12 medium-size, 1 large)
Shallots (4 large)
Baking potatoes (1½ pounds)
Fresh fruit (berries, apples, pears)
for cheese plate
Lemons (3 medium-size)

DAIRY

Large eggs (1 dozen)
Quail eggs or small chicken eggs (1 dozen)
Half-and-half (1 quart)
Heavy cream (2 quarts plus 1 pint)
Unsalted butter (1¼ pounds)
White cheddar cheese
(about ¼ pound)
Parmigiano-Reggiano cheese (about ¾ pound)
Assorted cheeses for cheese plate

FISH AND SEAFOOD COUNTER

Medium-size shrimp (1 pound)
Lump crabmeat (1 pound)
Shucked oysters (50)

MEAT DEPARTMENT

Domestic ducks (2, each about 5 pounds)
Raw chicken bones (8 pounds)
Bacon, sliced (¾ pound)
Andouille or kielbasa sausage (2 pounds)
Ham hocks (4 medium-sized, 3 pounds)

CONDIMENTS AND CANNED GOODS

Creole or whole-grain mustard
(3 tablespoons)
Worcestershire sauce (about 1¼ cups)
Tabasco sauce (½ teaspoon)
Soy sauce (¼ cup)

MISCELLANEOUS

Dried fine white bread crumbs (1½ cups)
White sliced bread (8 slices)
Dried black-eyed peas (1 pound)
Popcorn kernels (¼ cup)
French bread for cheese plate
Assorted nuts
Grand Marnier (¼ cup)
Heavy-duty aluminum foil

JIFFY POP FIRECRACKER SHRIMP

MAKES ABOUT 10 SERVINGS

1 pound medium-size shrimp, tails on,
   rinsed, patted dry, and peeled
1½ teaspoons salt
3 tablespoons Hot Pepper Oil
   (page 79)
¼ cup popcorn kernels
1 teaspoon Creole Seasoning
   (page 30)

Stocking Tip ■ For the best results, use a large nonstick skillet. If you don't use one, you run the risk of the spices burning.

Season the shrimp with ½ teaspoon of the salt and 1 tablespoon of the pepper oil.

Layer the shrimp in a concentric circle in the bottom of a cold 10- to 12-inch sauté pan, leaving about a 1-inch space between the shrimp and the rim of the pan. Drizzle the remaining 2 tablespoons pepper oil in this space around the inside of the pan. Sprinkle the popcorn kernels into the oil.

Cut a piece of heavy-duty aluminum foil about 14 inches long. Place the foil over the pan and press it down firmly over the shrimp, oil, and popcorn.

Crimp the foil securely around the edges of the skillet.

Put the pan over medium-high heat. Cook until it begins to sizzle, about 2 minutes. Continue to cook for about 2½ minutes more. The corn should begin popping. Start shaking the pan at 30-second intervals. The popcorn will continue to pop for about another 2 minutes. Turn off the heat. Let sit for about 30 seconds and allow the corn to completely finish popping.

Very carefully remove the foil because of the steam, pour the mixture into a large bowl, and toss it with the remaining teaspoon salt and the Creole seasoning. Serve immediately.

Spicy Crab Cakes with Fried Quail Eggs

MAKES 10 CAKES

2 tablespoons unsalted butter
1 cup finely chopped yellow onions
½ cup finely chopped celery
¼ cup seeded and finely chopped red
  bell pepper
¼ cup seeded and finely chopped
  yellow bell pepper
1½ teaspoons salt
¼ teaspoon cayenne
1 tablespoon chopped garlic
1 pound lump crabmeat, picked over for
  shells and cartilage
¼ cup chopped green onions
  (scallions), green parts only
¼ cup freshly grated Parmigiano-
  Reggiano cheese
2 tablespoons finely chopped fresh
  parsley leaves
3 tablespoons Creole or whole-
  grain mustard
3 tablespoons fresh lemon juice

2 large eggs
2 cups vegetable oil
¼ teaspoon freshly ground white pepper
½ teaspoon Worcestershire sauce
¼ teaspoon Tabasco sauce
1½ cups dried fine white bread crumbs
¼ cup bleached all-purpose flour
3 teaspoons Creole Seasoning
  (page 30)
1 tablespoon water
Fried Quail Eggs (page 99)
Creole Meunière Sauce (page 105)
Roasted Vegetable Pecan Relish
  (page 104)

Melt the butter in a small sauté pan over medium heat. Add the onions, celery, bell peppers, ½ teaspoon of the salt, and the cayenne. Cook, stirring, until the vegetables are soft and slightly golden, about 5 minutes. Add the garlic and cook, stirring, for 2 minutes. Cool for 5 minutes.

In a large mixing bowl, combine the crabmeat, green onions, cheese, parsley, mustard, and 2 tablespoons of the lemon juice. Mix well, then set aside.

In another bowl, whisk one of the eggs until frothy. Add the remaining tablespoon lemon juice, then slowly whisk in 1 cup of the vegetable oil. The mixture will look like thin mayonnaise. Add the white pepper, the remaining teaspoon salt, the Worcestershire, and Tabasco. Whisk together well.

Combine the vegetable mixture with the crab mixture. Fold in ½ cup of the mayonnaise mixture and ¾ cup of the bread crumbs. Mix well. Divide the mixture into 10 equal portions and form them into 1-inch-thick cakes (patties).

In a shallow bowl, combine the flour with 1 teaspoon of the Creole seasoning.

In another bowl, whisk the remaining egg with the water.

In a third bowl, combine the remaining ¼ cup bread crumbs and 1 teaspoon of the Creole seasoning.

Heat the remaining 1 cup oil to 360°F in a large sauté pan over medium-high heat.

Dredge the cakes first in the seasoned flour, tapping off any excess, then in the egg wash, letting the ex-

cess drip off. Dredge the cakes in the seasoned bread crumbs, coating them evenly. Gently lay the cakes, 3 or 4 at a time, in the oil and fry until lightly golden, about 4 minutes on each side. Drain on paper towels.

Season the cakes with the remaining teaspoon Creole seasoning. Serve each topped with a fried quail egg, dribbled with the meunière sauce and accompanied by the pecan relish.

FRIED QUAIL EGGS

MAKES 10 SERVINGS

1 tablespoon vegetable oil
10 quail eggs
Salt and freshly ground white
   pepper

Stocking Tip ■ Quail eggs can often be purchased from quail farmers and some specialty food shops. If quail eggs are unavailable, use small or medium-size chicken eggs. You will have to adjust the amount of vegetable oil for frying to 2 to 3 tablespoons.

Coat the bottom of a large nonstick skillet with the oil and heat over medium heat until the oil is hot but not smoking, about 1 minute. Gently crack each egg using the edge of a knife. Drop each egg in a small ramekin or cup and gently slide it into the hot oil. Cook three or four eggs at a time until they firm up, 1 to 1½ minutes. Larger eggs may take a little longer.

Transfer each egg to the top of a crab cake. Season each egg with a pinch of salt and pepper. Serve warm.

OYSTER AND PARSLEY CHOWDER WITH PARMESAN TUILES

MAKES 10 SERVINGS

¾ pound bacon, chopped (about 2 cups)
2 cups chopped yellow onions
1 cup chopped celery
1 cup chopped carrots
1½ teaspoons salt
½ teaspoon cayenne
6 bay leaves
¾ cup bleached all-purpose flour
8 cups Chicken Stock (page 30)
1½ pounds baking potatoes, peeled and
   diced (about 2 cups)
1 cup half-and-half
½ cup finely chopped fresh parsley
   leaves
50 shucked oysters with 1 cup oyster
   liquor
¼ teaspoon Tabasco sauce
1 teaspoon Worcestershire sauce
Parmesan Tuiles (page 104)

Stocking Tips ■ The soup can be cooked ahead of time. Follow the directions up to the point that the potatoes are cooked. The soup can be cooled, then refrigerated for up to 24 hours. When you are ready to complete it, warm the soup slowly and continue with the recipe. ■ It is very important not to overcook the oysters. Once they are added to the soup, they should be cooked only for 1 to 2 minutes, just until the edges curl, so that they are still plump and juicy.

Fry the bacon in a large nonstick stockpot over medium heat until slightly crisp. Add the onions, celery, carrots, salt, cayenne, and bay leaves and cook, stirring, until the vegetables are soft and tender, about 10 minutes. Add the flour and stir to blend. Cook until golden, about 10 minutes, stirring occasionally. Add the chicken stock and bring to a boil. Add the potatoes and simmer until they are fork-tender, about 15 minutes. Add the half-and-half and parsley and simmer for 5 minutes.

Add the oysters with their liquor, the Tabasco, and Worcestershire. Simmer until the edges of the oysters curl, about 2 minutes. Do not overcook the oysters. Remove the bay leaves and serve hot with the tuiles on the side.

CARAMELIZED ROASTED SKILLET DUCK WITH STEEN'S DUCK MARINADE

2 domestic ducks (each about 5 pounds)
¼ cup kosher salt
2 teaspoons cayenne
1 recipe Steen's Duck Marinade
  (page 105)

Stocking Tip ■ To cut the duck into eight pieces, remove the wings and legs, then the two breast sections, then the two thighs, leaving only the carcass. The carcass is excellent for making Duck Stock (page 57).

Cut each duck into eight pieces, reserving the carcass. Sprinkle the pieces with the salt and cayenne.

Divide the marinade into two equal portions. Pour each portion into a 1-gallon plastic bag. Divide the duck pieces equally between the bags. Seal and shake the bags to coat the duck pieces evenly with the marinade. Refrigerate for 24 hours, turning the bags over several times.

Drain the duck pieces in a colander, reserving the marinade. Pour the marinade into a saucepan and simmer over medium-low heat until it is thick and dark, about 30 minutes. Set aside.

Preheat the oven to 350°F.

Heat a large sauté pan over high heat with no oil. Add the duck pieces, skin side down, in batches, and sear until the skin is crisp, brown, and caramelized, about 4 minutes. Turn them over and sear for about 3 minutes. Transfer the pieces to a wire rack set in a baking pan lined with parchment or waxed paper. Bake for 35 minutes. Remove from the oven and smear all the pieces with the marinade. Return the duck to the oven and bake until the juices run clear, about another 15 minutes. Serve hot.

ROASTED VEGETABLE PECAN RELISH

1 large yellow squash (about ½ pound), cut lengthwise into 1-inch-thick slices

1 large zucchini (about ½ pound), cut lengthwise into 1-inch-thick slices

1 large eggplant (about ½ pound), cut lengthwise into 1-inch-thick slices

1 large yellow onion (about ¾ pound), thinly sliced

2 tablespoons minced garlic

2 tablespoons olive oil

1 teaspoon salt

½ teaspoon freshly ground black pepper

2 tablespoons unsalted butter

1 cup pecan halves

Preheat the oven to 350°F.

Combine the squash, zucchini, eggplant, onion, and garlic in a large mixing bowl. Add the oil, ½ teaspoon of the salt, and ¼ teaspoon of the pepper. Toss to coat evenly.

Put the mixture in a baking pan and roast until the vegetables are soft, about 30 minutes. Cool, then chop into ½-inch dice.

Combine the butter and pecans in a large nonstick skillet over high heat. Cook, stirring until they are toasted and golden brown, about 3 minutes. Add the vegetables and cook for about 1 minute, stirring once or twice. Add the remaining ½ teaspoon salt and ¼ teaspoon pepper and stir to mix. Serve hot.

PARMESAN TUILES

1¼ cup plus 2 tablespoons freshly grated Parmigiano-Reggiano cheese

Preheat the oven to 350°F.

Line a baking sheet with parchment or waxed paper. For each tuile, spread 3 tablespoons of the grated cheese on the paper to form a 3-inch round. Bake until golden brown, about 12 minutes.

Cool for 1 minute. Using a metal spatula, transfer the tuiles to another piece of parchment or waxed paper and cool completely. Use immediately or store in an airtight container for up to 24 hours.

CREOLE MEUNIÈRE SAUCE

1 cup Worcestershire sauce
½ cup chopped yellow onions
2 bay leaves
2 lemons, peel and pith discarded and
  cut in half
¾ cup heavy cream
1 pound (4 sticks) unsalted butter,
  cut into ½-inch chips
½ teaspoon Creole Seasoning
  (page 30)

Stocking Tip ■ "Mounting" is a cooking technique whereby small chips of cold butter are whisked into a sauce just before serving to give it flavor, texture, and a glossy appearance.

Combine the Worcestershire, onions, bay leaves, and lemons in a medium-size nonreactive saucepan over medium-high heat. Mash the lemons down with the back of a spoon and bring the mixture to a boil. Simmer until it has reduced and becomes slightly thick, 8 to 10 minutes. Add the cream and whisk to blend. Cook for 1 minute.

Mount in the butter, whisking constantly until it is completely melted and blended into the mixture. Add the Creole seasoning and stir to mix. Strain through a sieve and serve warm over the quail eggs on the crab cakes.

STEEN'S DUCK MARINADE

2 cups Steen's 100% Pure Cane Syrup
½ cup dark molasses
¼ cup soy sauce
¼ cup balsamic vinegar
½ cup water
2 tablespoons sesame oil
¼ cup minced shallots

2 tablespoons chopped garlic
2 tablespoons peeled and grated
  fresh ginger
1 teaspoon salt
½ teaspoon cayenne
¼ teaspoon freshly ground black
  pepper

Whisk all of the ingredients together in a mixing bowl, blending well. Pour the mixture into a sterilized 1-quart jar fitted with an airtight lid. Will keep in the refrigerator for 2 weeks.

CARAMELIZED ANDOUILLE SPOON BREAD

½ teaspoon unsalted butter

1 tablespoon vegetable oil

One 1-pound link andouille or kielbasa
    sausage, split in half lengthwise and
    cut crosswise into ¼-inch-thick slices
    (about 3½ cups)

1 cup finely chopped yellow onions

½ cup finely chopped celery

½ cup seeded and finely chopped green
    bell peppers

2 teaspoons salt

¼ teaspoon cayenne

1 tablespoon chopped garlic

2 tablespoons finely chopped fresh
    parsley leaves

¼ cup chopped green onions (scallions),
    green parts only

4 large eggs, separated

3 cups heavy cream

1½ cups yellow cornmeal

¼ cup freshly grated Parmigiano-
    Reggiano cheese

Preheat the oven to 350°F.

Grease a 2-quart rectangular glass dish (8 × 11½ × 2 inches) with the butter.

Heat the oil in a medium-size sauté pan over medium-high heat. Add the sausage and cook for 3 minutes, stirring occasionally. Add the onions, celery, bell peppers, salt, and cayenne and cook, stirring, until the vegetables are softened, about 5 minutes. Add the garlic and cook, stirring, for 1 minute. Remove from the heat and stir in the parsley and green onions. Cool the mixture for 10 minutes.

Whisk the egg yolks and cream together in a large mixing bowl. Add the cornmeal and whisk until the batter is smooth. Fold the sausage mixture into the batter.

In another large mixing bowl, whip the egg whites with an electric mixer until very stiff and peaks form, then fold into the sausage batter. Pour the batter into the prepared pan and sprinkle the top with the cheese. Bake until it sets, about 45 minutes.

Remove from the oven and let stand for 5 minutes. Spoon onto serving plate and serve warm.

Stewed Black-eyed Peas

One 1-pound link andouille or kielbasa
 sausage, sliced in half lengthwise and
 cut into ¼-inch-thick slices
 (about 3½ cups)
1 cup chopped yellow onions
½ teaspoon salt
¼ teaspoon cayenne
4 cloves garlic, peeled
5 sprigs fresh thyme
4 bay leaves
3 teaspoons finely chopped fresh parsley
 leaves
8 cups Chicken Stock (page 30)
1 pound dried black-eyed peas, rinsed,
 sorted over, soaked overnight in water
 to cover, and drained
1 tablespoon minced garlic

Brown the sausage in a large saucepan
over medium heat. Add the onions, salt,
cayenne, garlic cloves, thyme, bay leaves,
and parsley. Cook, stirring, until the
onions are wilted, about 5 minutes. Add
the stock, peas, and garlic. Bring the
mixture to a gentle boil, then reduce
the heat to medium-low and simmer,
uncovered, until the peas are tender,
about 1½ hours.

Remove the bay leaves and serve
warm.

COLLARD AND MUSTARD GREENS IN HAM HOCK GRAVY

MAKES 8 TO 10 SERVINGS

½ cup vegetable oil
½ cup bleached all-purpose flour
2 cups thinly sliced yellow onions
½ cup chopped celery
½ teaspoon salt
¼ teaspoon cayenne
4 bay leaves
2 tablespoons chopped garlic
8 cups Chicken Stock (page 30)
3 pounds ham hocks
   (about 4 medium-size hocks)
2 bunches (about 2¼ pounds) each of
   collards and mustard greens,
   thoroughly washed, picked over for
   blemished leaves, and tough stems
   removed
1 cup water

Stocking Tip ■ A roux is a mixture of oil and flour that, after being slowly cooked, is used to thicken mixtures such as soups and sauces. A blond roux is cooked until it is a pale golden color.

Combine the oil and flour in an 8-quart pot over medium heat and stir with a wooden spoon until smooth. Cook the mixture, stirring constantly, to make a blond roux, about 8 minutes.

Add the onions, celery, salt, cayenne, bay leaves, garlic, stock, and ham hocks. Bring the mixture to a boil, reduce the heat to medium-low, and simmer, uncovered, until the hocks are very tender, about 2 hours.

Add the greens, by the handful, until all of them are combined in the mixture. They will wilt. Add the water. Simmer until the greens are very tender and the mixture is thick, about 45 minutes.

Remove the bay leaves and serve warm.

JALAPEÑO AND CHEESE BISCUITS

*4 cups plus 2 tablespoons bleached
   all-purpose flour (about 1 pound)*
1½ tablespoons baking powder
*⅛ teaspoon freshly ground black
   pepper*
1 teaspoon salt
*2 fresh jalapeños, minced
   (about 2 tablespoons)*
1 cup grated white cheddar cheese
*1 cup plus 1 teaspoon vegetable
   shortening*
1½ cups half-and-half

Preheat the oven to 375°F.

Lightly grease a baking sheet with 1 teaspoon vegetable shortening.

Combine 4 cups of the flour, the baking powder, pepper, salt, jalapeños, and cheese in a large mixing bowl. Mix well. Add the shortening and work it into the dry ingredients, using your hands, until the mixture resembles coarse crumbs. Fold in the half-and-half. The dough will be sticky.

Dust your work surface with 1 tablespoon of the flour. Turn the dough onto the floured surface. Gently fold each side towards the center. Pick up the dough and dust the work surface with the remaining tablespoon flour. Return the dough to the floured surface and fold each side towards the center again. Turn the dough over and lightly press it out to 1-inch thickness. Cut the biscuits using a 2¼-inch round cookie cutter. Place them on the baking sheet and bake until golden, 30 minutes. Serve immediately.

ASSORTED CHEESE PLATE

A cheese course following a leisurely meal is always enjoyable especially at a holiday gathering. Here are a few tips. First, it's best to serve cheese at room temperature. Keep the cheese wrapped until ready to serve to prevent the surfaces from drying out. Allow one- to two-ounce chunks or slivers per person. Accompany the cheese with crusty bread, seasonal fruits such as sliced apples, pears, or berries, and nuts. Cheese plates often offer a blue cheese (Maytag blue, Danish blue, or the French Bleu de Bresse, or Stilton), a soft cheese (Camembert or Brie), and a hard cheese (Provolone, Pecorino, or Parmigiano-Reggiano).

You can experiment with the fruits and nuts you like to serve with a particular cheese, but here are some ideas. Toasted walnuts go well with blue cheese, as does fresh blueberries (especially with Bleu de Bresse). Serve strawberries with a creamy Brie. Fresh and juicy seasonal fruits, like apples and pears, can be served with most cheeses.

If locally made cheeses are available in your area, by all means, use them. In New Orleans, we are able to get local cheeses made by Chicory Farm in

nearby Mount Hermon. We like to call them *fromage de pays*, or the special cheese of the region. A plate of their cheeses (see Mail-Order Sources) is often served at Emeril's and our customers love it.

Chocolate Bread Pudding with Spiced Cream

1 teaspoon unsalted butter
4 large eggs
1 cup firmly packed light brown sugar
½ teaspoon ground cinnamon
⅛ teaspoon freshly grated nutmeg
1 teaspoon pure vanilla extract
1 cup semisweet chocolate chips, melted
¼ cup Grand Marnier or other orange-
   flavored liqueur
2 cups half-and-half
8 slices day-old white bread, crusts
   removed and cut into ½-inch cubes
   (about 4 cups)
2 cups semisweet chocolate chips
Spiced Cream (below)

Preheat the oven to 350°F.

Grease a 6-cup (9¼ × 5¼ × 2¼-inch) loaf pan with the butter.

Whisk the eggs, sugar, cinnamon, nutmeg, vanilla, melted chocolate, and Grand Marnier together in a large mixing bowl until very smooth. Add the half-and-half and mix well. Add the bread and let the mixture sit for 30 minutes, stirring occasionally.

Pour half of the mixture into the prepared pan. Sprinkle the top with the unmelted chocolate chips. Pour the remaining bread mixture over the chocolate chips. Bake until the pudding is set in the center, about 55 minutes. Let cool for 5 minutes.

To serve, cut the pudding into 1-inch-thick slices. Top with the spiced cream.

Spiced Cream

1 quart heavy cream
¼ cup granulated sugar
½ teaspoon ground cinnamon
¼ teaspoon freshly grated nutmeg

Beat the cream with an electric mixer on high speed in a large mixing bowl for about 2 minutes. Add the sugar, cinnamon, and nutmeg and beat again until the mixture thickens and forms stiff peaks, another 1 to 2 minutes.

CHEF'S
HOLIDAY
FAVORITES

IN LOUISIANA, WE ALWAYS

GIVE A little lagniappe, something extra. This section is my lagniappe to you. These are some of my all-time favorites that can be prepared anytime, not just during the holidays. Use these recipes for special

occasions like birthdays, anniversaries, family gatherings, or just to make something nice for someone who is very dear to your heart.

The spring rolls are great appetizers to serve prior to any meal.

The gumbo made with quail and smoked sausage or the Crab Bisque are especially good on a cold winter's

Shrimp Spring Rolls with Rice Wine and Soy Dipping Sauce

◆

Quail and Smoked Sausage Christmas Gumbo

◆

Lobster Cheesecake with Christmas Caviar Sauce

◆

Crab Bisque with Crab Boulettes

◆

Chicken and Andouille Strudel with Sweet Barbecue Sauce

◆

Peasant-style Tuna with Meat Juices and Fried Parsnips

Creamed Potatoes with Spinach and Roasted Garlic

◆

Smothered Veal Chops with Tasso Mushroom Gravy

◆

Crawfish Quiche

◆

Crabmeat Gratinée with Champagne Vanilla Sabayon

◆

Mirliton Gratin

night. The Lobster Cheesecake is ideal for a small supper party.

For a festive dinner, try the Smothered Veal Chops with Tasso Mushroom Gravy or the tuna served with creamed potatoes and spinach.

Heck, try them all to see which is your favorite.

Adieu!

Shrimp Spring Rolls with Rice Wine and Soy Dipping Sauce

MAKES 8 SERVINGS

10 cups water
1 lemon, halved
1¾ teaspoons salt
¼ teaspoon cayenne
1 tablespoon Zatarain's Concentrated
   Liquid Shrimp & Crab Boil (optional)
1 pound large shrimp, peeled, deveined,
   and tail removed
2 ounces Chinese cellophane or glass
   noodles
1 teaspoon sesame oil
1 teaspoon soy sauce
1 tablespoon chopped green onions
   (scallions), green parts only
⅛ teaspoon freshly ground black pepper
8 rice papers or spring roll wrappers
2 tablespoons plus 2 teaspoons hoisin
   sauce
4 large romaine leaves, cut in
   half vertically
½ cup radish, alfalfa, or bean sprouts
½ cup matchstick carrot strips
½ cup packed cilantro (fresh coriander)
   leaves, coarsely chopped
½ cup packed fresh mint leaves, coarsely
   chopped
Rice Wine and Soy Dipping Sauce
   (page 119)

Stocking Tips The rolls can be made a day ahead of time, then wrapped in plastic wrap and stored in the refrigerator. ■ Rice paper is an edible, translucent paper made from a dough of water combined with the pith of an Asian shrub called the rice paper plant. The paper comes in various sizes—small to large, round or square. Spring roll wrappers (or skins) are similar to won ton skins. Both can be found in the produce or refrigerated section of Asian markets and many supermarkets.

Put 4 cups of the water in a nonreactive medium-size saucepan over medium-high heat. Squeeze the lemon and add the juice and peel to the water. Add 1 teaspoon of the salt and the cayenne. Bring to a boil.

Season the shrimp with the shrimp and crab boil. Add the shrimp to the boiling water and cook for 2 minutes, stirring occasionally. Remove from the heat and let sit for 2 minutes. Drain and cool.

In another saucepan, combine 4 cups of the water and ½ teaspoon of the salt and bring to a boil. Add the noodles and boil until they are clear, about 2½ minutes, stirring occasionally. Drain and cool with cold water. Put the noodles in a small mixing bowl and toss with the sesame oil, soy sauce, the remaining ¼ teaspoon salt, the green onions, and black pepper.

Cut the shrimp in half lengthwise.

Bring the remaining 2 cups water to a boil in a 10-inch sauté pan and remove from the heat.

Line a baking sheet with parchment or waxed paper.

Submerge each spring roll wrapper, one at time, in the hot water, moving it around in the water until soft and pliable, 10 to 15 seconds. Remove and lay on the parchment paper.

Brush each wrapper with 1 teaspoon of the hoisin sauce. Lay a half leaf romaine in the center of each wrapper. On top of each half leaf, put 1 table-spoon of the noodle mixture and spread evenly. On top of the noodles, sprinkle 1 tablespoon of the sprouts. Top with 1 tablespoon of the carrots, 1 tablespoon of the cilantro, and 1 tablespoon of the mint. Lay 6 halves of shrimp next to each other on top of each mixture. Fold two sides of the wrapper toward the center about ¼ inch, then roll each like a jelly roll, pressing the edges together to seal. Repeat until all eight rolls are done.

When ready to serve, cut each roll in half diagonally. Serve chilled or at room temperature with the dipping sauce.

RICE WINE AND SOY DIPPING SAUCE

MAKES 2 CUPS

1 cup rice wine vinegar
2 tablespoons sesame oil
1 tablespoon soy sauce
3 tablespoons hoisin sauce
1 tablespoon minced shallots
1 teaspoon chopped garlic
2 tablespoons chopped green onions
  (scallions), green parts only
1 tablespoon chopped cilantro
  (fresh coriander) leaves
¼ cup chopped peanuts
¼ teaspoon salt
½ teaspoon red pepper flakes
½ carrot, cut into matchstick strips
  (about ¼ cup)

Whisk all of the ingredients together in a mixing bowl. Refrigerate the sauce in an airtight container for 2 hours before serving.

QUAIL AND SMOKED SAUSAGE CHRISTMAS GUMBO

MAKES 8 TO 10 SERVINGS

¾ cup vegetable oil

1 cup bleached all-purpose flour

2 cups chopped yellow onions

1 cup seeded and chopped green bell
   peppers

½ cup chopped celery

1 teaspoon salt

1 teaspoon cayenne

3 bay leaves

4 quail, about 3½ ounces each,
   breastbones removed

2 teaspoons minced garlic

8 cups Chicken Stock (page 30)

1 pound smoked sausage, cut crosswise
   into ¼-inch-thick slices

½ cup chopped green onions (scallions),
   green parts only

2 tablespoons finely chopped fresh
   parsley leaves

Stocking Tip ■ When making the roux, it is important that the oil-and-flour mixture be stirred constantly to keep it from burning.

Combine the oil and flour in a large nonstick saucepan over medium heat. Cook, stirring constantly, until the roux mixture is dark brown, the color of chocolate, 30 to 35 minutes.

Add the onions, peppers, celery, salt, cayenne, and bay leaves. Cook the vegetables, stirring often, until they are soft and tender, about 10 minutes.

Add the quail and garlic. Cook for about 5 minutes, turning the quail in the roux to coat evenly. Add the stock and sausage. Bring the mixture to a boil, then reduce the heat to medium-low, and simmer, uncovered, until the quail are very tender, about 1 hour.

Skim off any fat that rises to the surface of the gumbo and discard. Remove the bay leaves. Stir in the green onions and parsley. Serve immediately with steamed white rice.

Lobster Cheesecake with Christmas Caviar Sauce

MAKES ONE 9½-INCH CAKE; 16 SERVINGS

1 cup dried fine white bread crumbs
¾ cup freshly grated Parmigiano-
    Reggiano cheese
2 tablespoons unsalted butter, melted
1 tablespoon olive oil
1 cup finely chopped yellow onions
½ cup seeded and finely chopped red
    bell peppers
½ cup seeded and finely chopped yellow
    bell pepper
2 tablespoons minced shallots
1 tablespoon chopped garlic
¼ teaspoon Creole Seasoning
    (page 30)
2 pounds cream cheese, softened
6 large eggs
¾ cup heavy cream
¾ cup grated smoked Gouda cheese
¼ cup chopped green onions (scallions),
    green parts only
1 teaspoon salt
½ teaspoon Tabasco sauce
1 tablespoon Worcestershire sauce
¼ teaspoon cayenne
2 tablespoons finely chopped fresh
    parsley leaves

¾ pound cooked lobster tail meat,
    coarsely chopped
Christmas Caviar Sauce (page 58)

FOR GARNISH
Finely chopped red onions
Finely chopped hard-boiled egg whites
Finely chopped hard-boiled egg yolks
Capers, drained
Caviar

Preheat the oven to 350°F.

Combine the bread crumbs, ½ cup of the Parmigiano, and the butter in a small mixing bowl. Mix well. Using your fingers, press the mixture into the bottom of a 9½-inch springform pan. Bake until lightly browned, about 10 minutes. Remove from the oven and cool completely.

Heat the oil in a small sauté pan over medium heat. Add the onions and cook, stirring, for 1 minute. Add the bell peppers and cook, stirring, for 1 minute. Add the shallots and garlic and cook for 30 seconds. Stir in the Creole seasoning. Remove from the heat.

In a food processor, process the cream cheese until smooth. Add one egg at a time to the mixture, blending after each addition. With the machine running, add the cream, Gouda, and the remaining Parmigiano. Stop the machine and scrape down the sides of the container with a rubber spatula. Add the vegetable mixture, the green onions, salt, Tabasco, Worcestershire, cayenne, parsley, and lobster. Pulse the machine a few times to mix. Pour the mixture into the crust.

Bake until the cake sets, about 1 hour and 20 minutes. Remove from the oven and let the cake cool completely.

Place the cake in the refrigerator and chill for 8 hours. Remove the sides of the pan. Cut the cake into 16 slices. Spread a tablespoon of the caviar sauce on each serving plate. Top with a wedge of cake and garnish with the red onions, egg whites and egg yolks, capers, and caviar.

CRAB BISQUE WITH CRAB BOULETTES

MAKES 8 SERVINGS

¾ cup bleached all-purpose flour
¾ cup vegetable oil
1½ cups chopped yellow onions
½ cup seeded and chopped green bell
   peppers
½ cup chopped celery
½ cup chopped carrots
4 bay leaves
2½ teaspoons salt
½ teaspoon cayenne
6 gumbo crabs, each cut in half
1 cup peeled, seeded, and chopped fresh
   or canned tomatoes
½ cup brandy
8 cups water
1 teaspoon Zatarain's Concentrated
   Liquid Shrimp & Crab Boil
   (optional)
½ cup chopped green onions (scallions),
   green parts only
¼ cup finely chopped fresh parsley
   leaves
¼ cup heavy cream
1 pound lump crabmeat, picked over
   for shells and cartilage
Crab Boulettes (page 126)

Stocking Tips ■ Gumbo crabs are hard-shell crabs with the top half removed and the claws and legs attached. ■ To prepare the tomatoes, bring a pot of water to a boil. Make an X on the bottom of the tomatoes. Drop them into the boiling water and cook until the skins begin to shrivel, about 2 minutes. With a slotted spoon, transfer them to an ice water bath to cool. Remove the skins with a sharp knife and discard. Remove the seeds, then chop.

Combine the flour and oil in a large nonstick saucepan and whisk until smooth. Over medium heat, stir constantly until the mixture is the color of peanut butter, about 10 minutes.

Add the onions, bell peppers, celery, carrots, bay leaves, salt, and cayenne. Cook, stirring often, until the vegetables are soft, about 10 minutes.

Add the crabs and tomatoes and stir to mix. Cook for 10 minutes. Add the brandy, water, and Zatarain's boil. Bring to a boil. Reduce the heat to medium-low and simmer, uncovered, for 1 hour and 45 minutes.

Add the green onions and parsley. Remove the bay leaves. Remove from the heat and add the cream. Mix to blend.

Ladle into individual serving bowls and sprinkle each with ¼ cup crabmeat. Top each with a half crab and a crab boulette.

CRAB BOULETTES

MAKES 8 SERVINGS

½ pound lump crabmeat, picked over for
  shells and cartilage
1 cup cooked medium-grain white rice
¼ cup chopped onions
1 tablespoon chopped celery
1 tablespoon seeded and chopped green
  bell pepper
2 teaspoons minced garlic
2 teaspoons finely chopped fresh parsley
  leaves
2 teaspoons Creole or whole-grain
  mustard
2 tablespoons freshly grated
  Parmigiano-Reggiano cheese
2 tablespoons water
⅛ teaspoon Tabasco sauce
⅛ teaspoon Worcestershire sauce
¼ teaspoon salt
⅛ teaspoon cayenne
½ cup dried fine white bread crumbs
4 teaspoons Creole Seasoning
  (page 30)
1 large egg mixed with 1 tablespoon
  water
¼ cup bleached all-purpose flour
Vegetable oil for deep frying

Put the crabmeat, rice, onions, celery, bell pepper, garlic, parsley, mustard, cheese, water, Tabasco, Worcestershire, salt, and cayenne in a food processor. Process until the mixture is smooth but sticky, about 1 minute. Divide the crabmeat mixture into eight equal balls.

Combine the bread crumbs and 1 teaspoon of the Creole seasoning in a small bowl. In another bowl, put the egg mixture and 1 teaspoon of the Creole seasoning. In another bowl, combine the flour and another teaspoon Creole seasoning.

Heat 4 inches of oil, or enough to be able to submerge the boulettes, in a large pot or electric fryer to 360°F.

Dredge each ball in the flour mixture, tapping off any excess, then dip in the egg mixture, shaking off any excess. Dredge in the bread crumb mixture, coating the boulettes evenly.

Fry the balls, three or four at a time, until golden brown, 2 to 3 minutes. Remove and drain on paper towels.

Season the balls with the remaining teaspoon Creole seasoning. Serve with the crab bisque.

CHICKEN AND ANDOUILLE STRUDEL WITH SWEET BARBECUE SAUCE

MAKES 4 SERVINGS (3 PER SERVING)

1 tablespoon plus 2 teaspoons
  vegetable oil
1 boneless chicken breast (about
  6 ounces), skin removed, cut into
  ¼-inch dice
1 teaspoon Creole Seasoning
  (page 30)
4 ounces andouille or kielbasa sausage,
  cut into ¼-inch dice
½ cup chopped yellow onions
2 teaspoons chopped garlic
½ teaspoon salt
¼ teaspoon cayenne
¼ cup water
1¼ cups Sweet Barbecue Sauce
  (page 145)
1 tablespoon chopped fresh parsley
  leaves
3 tablespoons freshly grated
  Parmigiano-Reggiano cheese
2 tablespoons dried fine white bread
  crumbs
4 sheets phyllo dough

Stocking Tip ■ Keep the phyllo covered with a clean, damp cloth to prevent it from drying out while you work. The fresh dough is usually available in Greek markets. Frozen dough can be found in most supermarkets.

Heat 1 tablespoon of the oil in a 10-inch sauté pan over medium heat. Season the chicken with the Creole seasoning. Add the chicken dice and cook, stirring occasionally, for 2 minutes. Add the sausage and cook, stirring, for 2 minutes. Add the onions, garlic, salt, and cayenne and cook until the onions are very soft, about 5 minutes. Add the water, ½ cup of the barbecue sauce, the parsley, and cheese. Simmer for 1 minute. Remove from heat and add the bread crumbs. Mix well. Cool.

Stack the sheets of phyllo dough on top of each other and cut them into thirds. You will have a total of 12 sheets. Divide the sheets into four 3-sheet stacks. Lightly brush the top sheet of each stack with a teaspoon of vegetable oil. Put ¼ cup of the chicken mixture on the bottom edge of each oiled sheet. Fold in the ends toward the center about ¼ inch. Then, beginning at the bottom, roll up the phyllo securely, pressing to close. Lightly brush each strudel with the remaining oil.

Preheat the oven to 375°F.

Line a baking sheet with parchment or waxed paper. Place the strudels on the paper about 2 inches apart and bake until golden brown, about 15 minutes. Remove from the oven.

Cut each strudel in half diagonally and top with 1 tablespoon of the remaining barbecue sauce. Serve warm.

Peasant-style Tuna with Meat Juices and Fried Parsnips

MAKES 4 SERVINGS

4 tuna steaks, about 6 ounces each,
   about 1 inch thick
2 teaspoons Creole Seasoning
   (page 30)
3 tablespoons unsalted butter
1 cup chopped yellow onions
½ teaspoon salt
⅛ teaspoon cayenne
½ cup peeled, seeded, and chopped fresh
   or canned Italian plum tomatoes
¼ pound kalamata olives, pitted and
   halved (¾ cup)
¼ pound large green olives stuffed with
   pimientos, halved (¾ cup)
1 tablespoon chopped garlic
3 tablespoons chopped green onions
   (scallions), green parts only
1 tablespoon finely chopped fresh
   parsley leaves

1 tablespoon shredded fresh basil leaves
½ teaspoon chopped fresh thyme leaves
⅛ teaspoon freshly ground black pepper
1 cup Duck Stock (page 57)
Fried Parsnips (page 131)
Creamed Potatoes with Spinach and
   Roasted Garlic (page 130)

Season both sides of each tuna steak
with the Creole seasoning.

Heat a large sauté pan over high heat
for 2 minutes. Sear the steaks for
1 minute and turn over. Add 1 tablespoon of the butter, the onions, salt,
and cayenne. Cook for 1 minute and
remove the steaks.

Add another tablespoon of the butter to the pan and continue to cook the
onions for 3 minutes, stirring. Add the
tomatoes, olives, garlic, green onions,
herbs, and black pepper and cook, stirring, for 2 minutes. Add the stock and
bring to a boil. Reduce the heat
to medium-low and simmer for
1 minute. Return the tuna steaks to
the pan and add the remaining tablespoon butter. Cook for 1 minute, basting the steaks with the sauce. Remove
from the heat.

To serve, stack fried parsnips on top
of each tuna steak on individual plates
and serve with the creamed potatoes.

CREAMED POTATOES WITH SPINACH AND ROASTED GARLIC

MAKES 4 SERVINGS

*4 cups peeled and diced white potatoes
    (about 2 pounds)*
1½ teaspoons salt
¾ cup heavy cream
*¼ cup (½ stick) unsalted butter, cut
    into cubes*
1 head Roasted Garlic (page 131)
*2 cups thoroughly washed, stemmed,
    and roughly torn spinach*
*⅛ teaspoon freshly ground white
    pepper*

Combine the potatoes and 1 teaspoon of the salt in a large saucepan over medium heat. Cover the potatoes with water and cook until fork-tender, about 20 minutes. Drain.

Return the potatoes to the pan and, over low heat, stir them with a fork or wire whisk for about 2 minutes to dehydrate them. Add the cream, butter, garlic, and spinach. Stir to mix well. Add the remaining ½ teaspoon salt and the white pepper. Mix well. Serve immediately.

ROASTED GARLIC

1 head garlic
½ teaspoon olive oil
Pinch of salt
Pinch of freshly ground black pepper

Preheat the oven to 400°F.

Cut a small square of aluminum foil. Cut the garlic head in half and place on the foil. Drizzle both halves with the oil and season with the salt and pepper. Bring the ends of the foil together to make a small bag or pouch. Bake until the garlic is tender, about 45 minutes.

Remove the bag from the oven and carefully open it up a bit. Return to the oven for about 10 minutes more. Remove from the oven and let cool. Remove the flesh by squeezing each half clove between your thumb and index finger.

Use immediately or refrigerate in a little olive oil in an airtight container for 2 to 3 days.

FRIED PARSNIPS

MAKES 4 SERVINGS

1 large parsnip (4 to 5 ounces), peeled
Vegetable oil for deep frying
Salt

Using a vegetable peeler, cut paper-thin strips lengthwise from top to bottom of the parsnip, turning it as you work, making about 40 strips, about 10 strips per serving.

Heat 4 inches of oil in a large pot or electric fryer to 360°F.

Drop the strips, all at one time, into the hot oil. Be very careful as the hot oil may splatter. Using a slotted spoon or spatula, gently stir the strips around in the oil until golden brown, about 1 minute. Remove and drain on paper towels. Sprinkle with salt to taste.

Divide into four equal portions and stack on top of each tuna steak.

Smothered Veal Chops with Tasso Mushroom Gravy

4 double-cut veal loin chops
  (12 to 14 ounces each)
4 teaspoons Creole Seasoning
  (page 30)
¼ cup vegetable oil
¼ cup bleached all-purpose flour
2 medium-size yellow onions, thinly
  sliced (about 6 cups)
½ teaspoon salt
⅛ teaspoon cayenne
½ pound assorted exotic mushrooms,
  such as shiitakes, chanterelles, and
  oysters, wiped clean and chopped
  (about 3 cups)
2½ ounces tasso, chopped (about ½ cup)
1 tablespoon chopped garlic
2½ cups Chicken Stock (page 30)
1 tablespoon chopped fresh parsley
  leaves
3 tablespoons chopped green onions
  (scallions), green parts only
⅛ teaspoon freshly ground black
  pepper

Stocking Tip ■ Tasso is a heavily seasoned smoked ham used often in Louisiana for flavoring vegetables, stews, gumbos, and sauces. It can be found in some supermarkets. Spiced ham can be substituted.

Season the chops with the Creole seasoning, rubbing it in evenly.

Heat the oil in a large sauté pan over medium heat. Sear the chops until golden brown but not charred, 5 to 6 minutes, and turn over. Sear for 3 minutes on the second side for rare, or 5 minutes for medium-rare. Remove from the heat and transfer the chops to a heated platter.

Add the flour to the skillet and whisk until the mixture is smooth. Return to the heat. Cook, stirring constantly until the mixture is the color of chocolate, about 3 minutes. Add the onions, salt, and cayenne and cook for 2 minutes, stirring occasionally. Add the mushrooms, tasso, and garlic and cook, stirring, for 2 minutes. Add the stock, bring the mixture to a gentle boil, and simmer for about 2 minutes. Return the chops to the pan and simmer for 5 minutes, basting often. Remove from the heat and stir in the parsley, green onions, and black pepper.

Serve the chops warm with the pan gravy.

CRAWFISH QUICHE

MAKES ONE 9-INCH QUICHE; 8 SERVINGS

2½ cups plus 2 teaspoons bleached
    all-purpose flour
3¾ teaspoons salt
½ teaspoon plus ⅛ teaspoon cayenne
1 cup vegetable shortening
2 to 3 tablespoons ice water
1 tablespoon unsalted butter
¼ cup finely chopped yellow onion
3 tablespoons seeded and finely chopped
    red bell pepper
2 teaspoons chopped garlic
½ pound peeled crawfish tails
    (about 1 cup)
2 cups heavy cream
4 large eggs
¼ teaspoon Tabasco sauce
½ teaspoon Worcestershire sauce
2 tablespoons snipped fresh chives
3 tablespoons freshly grated
    Parmigiano-Reggiano cheese
1 cup grated white cheddar cheese

Stocking Tip ■ When preparing the pie crust, it's important that the dough not be overworked as it will become tough.

Combine 2½ cups flour, 2 teaspoons of the salt, and ¼ teaspoon of the cayenne in a mixing bowl. Cut in the shortening with a pastry blender or two knives until the mixture resembles coarse meal. Add the ice water and mix until the dough comes away from the sides of the bowl. Form the dough into a ball. Cover with plastic wrap and place in the refrigerator for at least 1 hour.

Preheat the oven to 350°F.

Remove the dough from the refrigerator and let sit for about 5 minutes. Lightly dust a work surface. Roll the dough out into a 12-inch round about ¼ inch thick. Fold the dough into fourths and place it in a 10-inch quiche pan. Press the dough, using your fingers, firmly into the bottom and sides of the pan. Roll a wooden rolling pin over the pan to cut off the excess dough. Prick the bottom of the crust all over with a fork.

Melt the butter in a medium-size sauté pan over medium heat. Add the onion, bell pepper, garlic, 1 teaspoon of the salt, and ¼ teaspoon of the cayenne and cook, stirring, until the vegetables are soft, about 4 minutes. Add the crawfish tails and cook, stirring, for 2 minutes. Remove from the heat and let cool.

In a large mixing bowl, whisk together the cream, eggs, the remaining ¾ teaspoon salt, the remaining ⅛ teaspoon cayenne, the Tabasco, Worcestershire, chives, and Parmigiano. Pour the crawfish mixture into the pastry shell. Sprinkle the top with the cheddar. Pour the cream mixture over the crawfish mixture. Bake until the center sets and the top is golden, about 55 minutes.

Remove from the oven and let cool for 5 minutes before slicing to serve.

CRABMEAT GRATINÉE WITH CHAMPAGNE VANILLA SABAYON

½ teaspoon unsalted butter
1 pound lump crabmeat, picked over
    for shells and cartilage
½ teaspoon salt
¼ teaspoon freshly ground white
    pepper
2 teaspoons snipped fresh chives
¼ cup freshly grated Parmigiano-
    Reggiano cheese
¼ cup dried fine white bread crumbs
1 recipe Champagne Vanilla Sabayon
    (below)

Preheat the oven to 400°F. Butter a gratinée dish.

Combine the crabmeat, salt, pepper, chives, cheese, and bread crumbs in a large mixing bowl and mix well. Spoon the mixture into the gratinée dish and distribute evenly. Spoon the sabayon over the mixture. Bake until the top is golden brown, about 8 minutes.

CHAMPAGNE VANILLA SABAYON

MAKES ABOUT ¾ CUP

3 large egg yolks
2 teaspoons minced shallots
¼ teaspoon pure vanilla extract
¼ cup Champagne
¼ teaspoon salt
⅛ teaspoon freshly ground white
    pepper
1 teaspoon snipped fresh chives

Combine all of the ingredients in a small stainless-steel bowl. Set the bowl over a pot of simmering water and whisk until the mixture begins to thicken, about 2 minutes. Remove from heat.

MIRLITON GRATIN

1 tablespoon unsalted butter
4 mirlitons (about 2¼ pounds)
6 cups water
3 bay leaves
1 tablespoon plus ½ teaspoon salt
¼ teaspoon cayenne
1 tablespoon Zatarain's Concentrated
  Liquid Shrimp & Crab Boil
  (optional)
¼ pound andouille or kielbasa sausage,
  finely chopped
¼ cup olive oil
2 cups thinly sliced yellow onions
⅛ teaspoon freshly ground black pepper
2 teaspoons chopped garlic
1 tablespoon chopped fresh parsley
  leaves
2 tablespoons chopped green onions
  (scallions), green parts only
¾ cup dried fine white bread crumbs
½ cup freshly grated Parmigiano-
  Reggiano cheese
1 tablespoon Creole Seasoning
  (page 30)

Stocking Tip ■ Mirliton is also known as chayote, vegetable pear, christophine, or cho-cho. The firm white flesh, surrounding a single pear seed, has a delicate flavor. This gourdlike fruit is about the size and shape of a very large pear. It can be found in some supermarkets throughout the year.

Preheat the oven to 350°F.

Grease a 2-quart rectangular baking pan with the butter.

In a large saucepan, combine the mirlitons, water, bay leaves, 1 tablespoon of the salt, the cayenne, and Zatarain's boil, if using. Bring to a boil over medium-high heat and cook, uncovered, until the mirlitons are fork-tender, about 40 minutes.

Remove from the heat and drain. Let cool for 30 minutes and peel. Cut the mirlitons in half lengthwise and remove the seeds. Cut each half into ½-inch-thick slices.

In a large sauté pan over medium heat, brown the sausage about 4 minutes. Transfer to a small bowl.

To the same sauté pan, add 2 tablespoons of the olive oil. Add the onions, the remaining ½ teaspoon salt, and the black pepper. Cook, stirring, until the onions are soft and lightly golden, about 5 minutes. Add the mirlitons, garlic, parsley, and green onions; cook, stirring, for 2 minutes, and remove from the heat. Pour the mixture into the prepared pan.

Combine the sausage, bread crumbs, cheese, Creole seasoning, and the remaining 2 tablespoons olive oil. Mix well. Sprinkle the mixture over the mirliton mixture, covering the top completely. Bake until the top is golden brown, about 30 minutes. Serve warm.

EMERIL'S
STOCKING
STUFFERS

AS YOU MIGHT EXPECT,

FOODSTUFFS ARE my favorite gifts. Food is great for gift-giving. You don't have to know what size or color to get, and no one will have to stand in line to return it. My mother is responsible for teaching me

that homemade gifts are usually far more appreciated than an expensive bauble purchased at the last minute.

For weeks before the holidays, my kitchen is Santa's workshop. Like Mama, I begin gathering ingredients right after Thanksgiving. I stockpile nuts, sugar, and flour. Unusual bottles, festive tins, and baskets are gathered and stored in a seldom-used closet until I need them. Then I begin a list of all the people who are near and dear to me. Family members of course are at the top of the list, but then there are close friends, neighbors, distant cousins, my barber, the postman, and the shoeshine guy, and I'm always prepared for un-

STOCKING STUFFERS

....

Emeril's Homemade Worcestershire Sauce (page 29)
Hot Pepper Oil (page 79)
Roasted Pepper Ketchup
Sweet Barbecue Sauce
Steen's Duck Marinade (page 105)
Chocolate Macadamia Nut Brittle
Pickled Jalapeños
Creole Seasoning (page 30)
Orange Pralines
Butter Cream Mints
Mixed Nut Brittle
Christmas Lollipops
Chocolate Truffles (page 89)
Big Boy Cookies (page 63)
Three-tiered Braided Christmas Bread
Creole Christmas Fruitcake with Whiskey Sauce (page 61)

expected visitors who drop by for a glass of cheer or a cup of coffee.

My philosophy is to make more than you think you will need. Nothing will go to waste. Whether you have a big kitchen or just a small one, invite a few friends or family members to help you. I guarantee puttering around in the kitchen will get everyone in a festive spirit. The aromas emanating from your kitchen will make your neighbors pea green with envy!

Which reminds me of a story Marcelle told me. When she was in grade school, she was taught by nuns belonging to the Order of Mercy. Each year, soon after Thanksgiving, they would is-

sue a letter to parents asking for donations of canned milk, pecans, sugar, flour, and other ingredients. These were used by the nuns to make all sorts of Christmas treats, like pralines, fudge, lemon tarts, and assorted small cakes.

The nuns' house was located in the center of town, next to the old school, which was once a hotel. Late in the afternoons, passersby could hear pots banging and clanging in the large kitchen of the big house while the nuns sang Christmas hymns. The aromas from the kitchen perfumed the air. Young children sometimes slipped out of nearby homes and hid in the bushes to watch the nuns at work. Then, right before Christmas, the nuns would have what was called a Christmas Tree, an all-day fund-raising party. Small booths were erected in the schoolyard and the nuns sold their goodies to make money to buy books for the school. In turn, the treats were so sought after, they were given as gifts during the holidays.

Nice story, don't you think?

Let's see, back to our gifts. Be sure to pack cookies, candies, cakes, and pralines in decorative airtight tins to keep them fresh. Items like the Creole Seasoning, Hot Pepper Oil, and Roasted Pepper Ketchup can go in odd-shaped or colorful bottles. Tie the neck of the bottles with gay ribbons

and attach a recipe or two with them. Deliver the Three-tiered Braided Christmas Bread warm and fresh from the oven if possible.

Remember, this is the time for giving. Be assured, you will get a lot of satisfaction in knowing that these gifts will bring both the giver and the receiver a little glow. Enjoy!

ROASTED PEPPER KETCHUP

MAKES 1 QUART

5 large tomatoes (about 3 pounds),
   cored and quartered
2 medium-size yellow onions
   (about 1 pound), quartered
5 large red bell peppers
   (about 1¼ pounds)
3 poblano peppers (about ½ pound)
8 garlic cloves, peeled
2 tablespoons olive oil
4 teaspoons salt
½ teaspoon freshly ground black pepper
¼ teaspoon cayenne
¼ cup distilled white vinegar
¼ cup cider vinegar
¼ teaspoon Tabasco sauce
1 teaspoon Worcestershire sauce
2 tablespoons molasses

Preheat the oven to 400°F.

In a large mixing bowl, toss the tomatoes, onions, peppers, and garlic with the olive oil, 1 teaspoon of the salt, and the black pepper. Spread the mixture on a baking sheet and roast until everything is very soft, about 1 hour.

Remove from the oven. Return the mixture to the mixing bowl, cover with plastic wrap, and let cool for 45 minutes.

Drain and reserve the liquid. Peel off the skin of all the peppers, cut open, and remove the seeds.

Process the vegetables together in a food processor until smooth. Add the remaining ingredients plus ½ cup reserved liquid and process until blended.

Sterilize a quart-size preserving jar and keep hot. Sterilize the lid and keep hot. Pour the mixture into the jar leaving ½-inch head space at the top. With a clean damp towel, wipe the rim and fit with the hot lid. Tightly screw on the metal ring and place the jar on a rack in a deep canning kettle with boiling water to cover by 1 inch. Cover the kettle and boil for 15 minutes. Using tongs, remove the jar, place on a towel, and let cool. During the heat processing, the contents of the jar expand, forcing some of the air out. The remaining air inside contracts as it cools to create a partial vacuum, which pulls the lid tight against the jar rim. The vacuum and the lid's sealing compound maintain the seal. A popping noise after the contents have cooled is an indication that the seal is complete. To test, press the center of the cooled lid. If it stays depressed, the jar is sealed. If not, refrigerate and use the contents within 2 to 3 weeks or reseal with a new flat lid and repeat the hot water bath. Tighten the ring. Let stand in a cool, dry place for at least 2 weeks before using. Refrigerate once opened; the ketchup will keep up to one month.

SWEET BARBECUE SAUCE

Two 14-ounce bottles tomato ketchup
¾ cup water
1 tablespoon molasses
1 tablespoon Creole or whole-grain
    mustard
1 tablespoon chopped garlic
½ cup chopped yellow onions
¼ cup firmly packed light brown sugar
1 teaspoon Tabasco sauce
1 teaspoon Worcestershire sauce
½ teaspoon salt
¼ teaspoon cayenne
1 tablespoon peeled and grated fresh
    ginger
¼ teaspoon freshly ground black pepper

Combine all of the ingredients in a food processor or blender and process until smooth, about 15 seconds. Scrape down the sides of the bowl with a rubber spatula. Pulse two or three times.

Sterilize a quart-size preserving jar and keep hot. Sterilize the lid and keep hot. Pour the mixture into the jar, leaving ½-inch head space at the top. With a clean, damp towel, wipe the rim and fit with the hot lid. Tightly screw on the metal ring and place the jar on a rack in a deep canning kettle with boiling water to cover by 1 inch. Cover the kettle and boil for 15 minutes. Using tongs, remove the jar, place on a towel, and let cool. During the heat processing, the contents of the jar expand, forcing out some of the air. The remaining air inside contracts as it cools to create a partial vacuum, which pulls the lid tight against the jar rim. The vacuum and the lid's sealing compound maintain the seal. A popping noise after the contents have cooled is an indication that the seal is complete. To test, press the center of the cooled lid. If it stays depressed, the jar is sealed. If not, refrigerate and use the contents within 2 to 3 weeks or reseal with a new flat lid and repeat the hot water bath. Tighten the ring and store in a cool, dry place. Let stand for at least 2 weeks before using. Refrigerate once opened; the sauce will keep up to one month.

Chocolate Macadamia Nut Brittle

MAKES ABOUT 1 ¼ POUNDS

3 cups semisweet chocolate chips
   (about 1 pound)
2 tablespoons unsalted butter
One 4.5-ounce can macadamia nuts
   (about 1 cup)

Line a baking sheet with parchment or waxed paper.

Put the chocolate chips and 1 tablespoon of the butter in a stainless-steel bowl set over a pot of simmering water over medium heat. Stirring, melt the chocolate, about 5 minutes.

Heat the remaining tablespoon butter in a small skillet over medium-high heat. Add the nuts and shake the pan often to lightly toast them, 3 to 4 minutes. Add the nuts to the chocolate and cook, stirring the mixture often, until the chocolate is completely melted and the nuts are well coated, about 5 minutes.

Pour the chocolate mixture into the pan and spread it evenly with a rubber spatula over the bottom, making a ¼-inch-thick layer. Cool. Refrigerate until it sets, about 2 hours.

Break it into pieces, like peanut brittle. Store in an airtight container in the refrigerator. It will keep up to 2 weeks.

PICKLED JALAPEÑOS

MAKES ABOUT I QUART

1½ pounds fresh jalapeños
  (about 32)
2 teaspoons Zatarain's Concentrated
  Liquid Shrimp & Crab Boil
  (optional)
1 quart distilled white vinegar
1 tablespoon black peppercorns
6 bay leaves
2 tablespoons salt
12 cloves garlic, peeled

Stocking Tip ■ Zatarain's Concentrated Liquid Shrimp & Crab Boil is available at some seafood markets or can be ordered by calling The New Orleans School of Cooking and Louisiana General Store, (800) 237-4841.

Combine all of the ingredients in a nonreactive 2-quart saucepan over medium heat. Simmer until the peppers are very soft, about 25 minutes. Remove from the heat and let steep for 30 minutes, then remove the bay leaves.

Sterilize a quart-size jar and lid. Pour the mixture into the jar and secure with an airtight lid. Store in a cool, dry place for at least 2 weeks before using. Once opened, it will keep up to one month in the refrigerator.

ORANGE PRALINES

1 quart heavy cream
2¼ cups granulated sugar
1 orange
1 tablespoon light corn syrup
1½ cups pecan pieces

Cover a countertop with two or three sheets of parchment or waxed paper.

Pour the cream and sugar into a large, heavy-bottomed pot. Grate the rind of the orange over the pot. Add the corn syrup and pecan pieces. Over medium heat, stir the mixture often until it becomes very thick and a candy thermometer registers 275°F, about 1 hour.

Remove the pot from the heat. Drop the mixture by the tablespoon, onto the parchment paper, working quickly. Cool completely.

Lift the pralines off the paper with a thin knife. Store in an airtight container between layers of parchment paper at room temperature for up to 2 weeks.

BUTTER CREAM MINTS

10⅔ tablespoons unsalted butter,
   at room temperature
1 pound confectioners' sugar, sifted
1 teaspoon pure mint extract

Cream the butter in a large mixing bowl with an electric mixer on low speed until it is soft and fluffy. Add the sugar and the mint extract and beat at low speed until the mixture is thick, creamy, and smooth. Scrape down the sides of the bowl.

Cut two large sheets of plastic wrap and place on your work surface.

Divide the mixture into two equal portions and place each on the plastic sheets. Roll the mixture into the plastic wrap, forming it into logs about ½ inch in diameter. Wrap the plastic wrap securely around the logs and chill for 4 hours.

Pinch off about a rounded teaspoon of the butter cream and shape into 1-inch balls. Place the balls on parchment or waxed paper and flatten with the tines of a fork.

Refrigerate in layers of parchment paper in an airtight container until ready to serve. Will keep for up to 1 week.

MIXED NUT BRITTLE

2 cups water

4 cups granulated sugar

2 cups light corn syrup

1 tablespoon Steen's 100% Pure Cane Syrup

2 teaspoons salt

4 cups assorted nuts, such as pine nuts, pecan pieces, walnut pieces, sliced almonds, and peanuts

¼ cup (½ stick) unsalted butter, at room temperature

½ teaspoon baking soda

Line two baking sheets with parchment or waxed paper.

Combine the water and sugar in a large nonstick heavy-bottomed saucepan over medium-high heat. Stir to dissolve the sugar, 4 to 5 minutes. Add the corn syrup, cane syrup, and salt, and stir constantly and slowly with a wooden spoon until the mixture comes to a gentle boil, about 12 minutes. Continue stirring until the mixture reaches between 225° and 230°F on a candy thermometer.

Add the nuts and continue stirring until the mixture reaches 290°F. Remove the pan from the heat. Add the butter and baking soda and stir until the butter is completely melted, about 1 minute. Pour the mixture onto the baking sheets, being careful as it is very hot, and spread it evenly with a rubber spatula. Let cool completely.

Break into pieces and store in an airtight container. Will keep for up to 2 weeks.

CHRISTMAS LOLLIPOPS

MAKES ABOUT 3 DOZEN

1 pound white chocolate, broken into
    small pieces
¼ cup finely chopped walnuts
1 teaspoon unsalted butter
36 candy stick molds
36 swizzle sticks (or candy sticks)

Stocking Tips ■ Use a fine-quality white chocolate that is made with cocoa butter rather than vegetable oil. ■ If you don't want to mold the chocolate, wrap the mixture in plastic wrap, roll it into a log, refrigerate it until firm, then cut into slices. ■ Finely chopped pecans or macadamias can be substituted for the walnuts. ■ To add a festive touch, use clear swizzle sticks in which to set the chocolate. Decorate the sticks with tiny red, green, and gold ribbons.

Combine the chocolate and nuts in a stainless-steel bowl set over a pan of simmering water. Stir the mixture with a wooden spoon until the chocolate melts and is creamy and smooth. Add the butter and stir to melt.

Spoon about 1 tablespoon of the mixture into the molds fitted with the sticks. Smooth out the top of each candy with a thin knife. Chill until the candy sets, 2 to 3 hours.

Remove the candy from the molds and store in layers of parchment or waxed paper in an airtight container. Will keep for up to 2 weeks.

THREE-TIERED BRAIDED CHRISTMAS BREAD

MAKES 1 LARGE BRAIDED BREAD

SUN-DRIED TOMATO PASTE
1 cup water
¼ cup whole sun-dried tomatoes
3 tablespoons olive oil
2 teaspoons chopped garlic
¼ teaspoon salt
¼ teaspoon freshly ground black pepper

PESTO
1 cup lightly packed fresh basil leaves
2 tablespoons pine nuts
½ teaspoon chopped garlic
¼ teaspoon freshly ground black pepper
¼ teaspoon salt
3 tablespoons olive oil
*2 tablespoons freshly grated
   Parmigiano-Reggiano cheese*

TAPENADE
*20 kalamata olives (about ¾ cup),
   pitted*
1 anchovy fillet
2 teaspoons chopped garlic
2 tablespoons olive oil
¼ teaspoon freshly ground black pepper

Stocking Tips ■ Each of the tiers is flavored with a different mixture—tapenade, pesto, or sun-dried tomato paste. Prepare these in advance so that they will be ready to add to each batch of dough. ■ If you purchase sun-dried tomatoes packed in oil, drain the tomatoes well and press out the excess oil before using. ■ To remove the pits from the kalamata olives, wrap them in a sheet of paper toweling and gently hammer with a meat mallet. Unwrap the paper towel. The pits can then be easily removed. ■ If you don't wish to braid the bread, bake each loaf separately, 25 to 30 minutes.

DOUGH (YOU WILL NEED TO MAKE THREE BATCHES OF THIS DOUGH)
1 envelope (¼ ounce) dry yeast
1 tablespoon granulated sugar
1 cup warm water (about 110°F)
1 teaspoon salt
3½ cups bleached all-purpose flour
1 teaspoon vegetable oil
1 large egg, beaten
3 teaspoons kosher salt
*¼ teaspoon coarsely ground black
   pepper*

TO MAKE THE TOMATO PASTE: Combine the water and tomatoes in a small saucepan over medium-high heat. Bring to a boil and cook until softened, about 5 minutes. Drain well. Transfer to a food processor or blender, add the olive oil, garlic, salt, and pepper, and process. Purée until the mixture is smooth, about 15 seconds. Set aside.

TO MAKE THE PESTO: Combine all the ingredients in a food processor or blender and process until the mixture is smooth, about 15 seconds. Set aside.

TO MAKE THE TAPENADE: Combine all its ingredients in a food processor or blender and process until the mixture is smooth, about 15 seconds. Set aside.

TO MAKE THE DOUGH: Combine the yeast, sugar, and water in the bowl of an electric mixer fitted with a dough hook. Beat on low speed for 1 minute. Add the sun-dried tomato paste (or pesto or tapenade), salt, and flour. Beat at low speed until all of the flour is incorporated, about 1 minute. Then beat at medium speed until the mixture forms a ball, leaves the sides of the bowl, and climbs up the dough hook.

Remove the dough from the bowl. Using your hands, form the dough into a smooth ball. Lightly oil a bowl. Place the dough in the bowl and turn it to oil all sides. Cover with plastic wrap and set aside in a warm, draft-free place until it doubles in size, about 1 hour.

Preheat the oven to 350°F.

TO ASSEMBLE: Remove the dough from the bowl and invert it onto a lightly floured surface. Pat the dough into a rectangle about ¼ inch thick. Roll up the dough, beginning with the short side and stopping after each full turn to press the edge of the roll firmly into the flat sheet of dough to seal. Press with your fingertips. Tuck and roll so that any seams disappear into the dough.

Join the ends of each bread loaf and pinch all three together. Begin braiding, lapping each loaf one at a time over the other, then pinch the remaining ends together. Tuck the pinched ends underneath the braided bread.

Line a baking sheet with parchment or waxed paper. Place the bread on the baking sheet. Cover with plastic wrap and set aside in a warm, draft-free place until it doubles in size, about 1 hour.

Preheat the oven to 350°F.

With a pastry brush, brush the beaten egg evenly over the bread. Combine the kosher salt and pepper and sprinkle over the top of the bread. Bake until lightly brown, 45 to 50 minutes. Remove from the oven and cool on a rack.

MAIL-ORDER SOURCES

Cane River Pecan Co.
(318) 367-3226
Cracked pecans, pecan pieces, shelled pecan halves

Charlie Trotter's Citrus Cured
   Smoked Salmon
Charlie Trotter's Restaurant
816 West Armitage
Chicago, IL 60614
(773) 248-6228
*Available in 4 ounces, 6 ounces, 1 pound,
   or whole sides*

Chicory Farms
(504) 877-4550
P.O. Box 25
Mount Hermon, LA 70450
Exotic mushrooms and local gourmet cheeses

The C. S. Steen Syrup Mill, Inc.
(318) 893-1654 or (800) 725-1654
Steen's 100% Pure Cane Syrup

Essence of Emeril Spice Pack
New New Orleans Cooking Cookbook
Louisiana Real & Rustic Cookbook
Emeril's Homebase
638 Camp Street
New Orleans, LA 70130
(504) 524-4241 or visit us at our website at
   http;\\www.emerils.com

Konriko Company Store
(800) 551-3245
Rice, Konriko Brand wild pecan rice, spices

Maytag Cheese Company
(800) 247-2458
Maytag blue cheese

New Orleans Fish House
(504) 821-9700 or (800) 839-3474
Crawfish, shrimp, crabmeat, wasabi-
   injected roe

Sugar Cane Swizzle Sticks
Frieda's, Inc.
P.O. Box 58488
Los Angeles, CA 90058

Urbani Truffle USA
(800) 281-2330
Truffle oil

INDEX